PERSUASION AND DARK PSYCHOLOGY

DARK SECRETS OF PSYCHOLOGY AND THE ART OF INFLUENCING PEOPLE WITH PERSUASION TECHNIQUES, NLP NEURO LINGUISTIC PROGRAMMING AND HYPNOTISM.

Table of Contents

Introduction... 1

Chapter 1 What Is Persuasion 3

Chapter 2 Advanced Persuasion Techniques........................ 13

Chapter 3 Difference Between Persuasion And Manipulation. 21

Chapter 4 The Psychology Of Persuasion 38

Chapter 5 Mind Control With NLP To Get What You Want 51

Chapter 6 Protecting Oneself from NLP Mind Control 61

Chapter 7 What Is Dark Psychology And How To Use It To Influence People 74

Chapter 8 How To Hypnotize A Person 77

Chapter 9 Other Benefits of Hypnosis.................................. 95

Chapter 10 What Is The Dark Triad Psychology? (Narcissism, Machiavellianism, And Psychopathy) 102

Chapter 11 Dark Triad Axis and Application 115

Chapter 12 Speed Reading People.................................. 122

Conclusion 128

Introduction

Welcome to the world of dark psychology. While it may be scary to delve into at first, this is your ultimate manual for safe passage from beginning to end. You may be wondering what, exactly, "dark" psychology is... and is it as menacing as it sounds?

The short answer is "sometimes". Of course, we'll delve into the specifics later on! For now, understand that it refers to our predisposition to manipulate and prey on others. It's important to understand the reasoning behind criminal minds and how you can protect yourself from these master manipulators.

Mind control, coercion, and manipulation are three of the key ingredients in cooking up dark psychological schemes. Criminology is deeply related to it because of this. If you're interested in true crime you've landed upon the right book.

Have you ever heard of "The Dark Triad"? It's central to the theme of dark psychology. This refers to the three worst traits to see in a person: Narcissism, Machiavellianism, and Psychopathy. Each has a crucial role to play in understanding the mechanisms of dark psychology, who uses these methods, and how they affect your everyday life.

People around the world have been practicing the science of Psychology for, basically, ever. Understanding the human mind and what makes it tick is no easy task. Over the course of time the thoughts and ideas in the world of Psychology have changed drastically. Many people rely on Psychologists to help them understand their behavior. In addition, they rely on them to help them figure out ways to deal with the problems of the world that weigh them down.

Most people know that there are many types of Psychologists. You may have even spent some time with one in the past to work on your family, marriage, daily struggles, or issues that are much more sinister in nature. Psychology is not an exact science and what will work for some will not work for others. It is an ever-evolving science that can be very difficult to understand.

Chapter 1 What Is Persuasion

Persuasion is a theme of dark psychology that can be said to share quite a bit of similarity to manipulation. This is because they are both deployed in order to influence the motivations, behaviors, attitudes, and beliefs of a particular victim. There are a number of reasons why we adopt persuasion into our everyday lives, but the main one would have to be to get people with different ideas on the same page. In company, for instance, the persuasion method will be used to alter the attitude of a person towards an item, concept, or a particular event that is taking place. Either written or spoken phrases will be used during the process to express the other person's thinking, emotions, or data. Another common instance you can use persuasion is to fulfil a private benefit. This would include either advocacy for trial when providing a pitch for sales or during an election campaign. Although none of these are deemed to be good or evil, they are still used to affect the listener to behave or believe in some manner.

One understanding of persuasion is that it utilizes one's private or positional resources to alter other people's attitudes or behaviors. There are also several distinct kinds of persuasion recognized; the process of altering views or attitudes by appealing to reason and logic is known as systematic persuasion; the process of altering views and attitudes by appealing to feelings or practices is known as heuristic persuasion.

Persuasion is a type of mind control that is constantly being used in society. You may attempt to convince them to believe the same way you do when you speak to someone about politics. You are persuaded to vote a certain way when you listen to a political campaign. There's a lot of persuasion going on when someone is attempting to sell you a fresh item. This form of mind control is so prevalent that most people don't even know it's happening at all to them. The problem will arise when someone takes the time to convince you to believe ideals and values that do not suit your own value system. There are many distinct types of persuasion available. Not all of them have a bad intention, but they will all work to get the subject to change their minds about something. When a political candidate arrives on television, on Election Day they try to get the topic, or the voter, to vote on the ballot a certain way. The company that submitted that advertisement is attempting to get the victim to buy that item when you see a commercial on television or online. All of these are kinds of persuasion that are bent on attempting to modify the way they believe about the victim. To get the victim to modify their way of thinking. Dark persuasion has no moral motivation whatsoever. The motivation is rather amoral and sometimes largely immoral. If beneficial conviction is understandable as assisting individuals to help themselves, dark persuasion can be seen as a mechanism by which individuals behave against their own self-interest. Sometimes people make it reluctantly, knowing that they may not make the best choice, but are keen to stop the continuous persuasion efforts. On other occasions, the best dark persuaders can make someone think they act wisely when they actually do just the opposite.

So, what are the primary reasons for these dark persuaders? It depends on the type of person who persuades. Some people try to convince others to serve their own interests. Others do pure harm by the sole malicious intent. They may not profit from persuading anyone, but they do it anyhow, solely in order to bring pain to their victims. Others just appreciate the feeling of control provided by dark persuasion.

The result of dark persuasion is also different from positive persuasion. Positive persuasion usually results in one of three scenarios: benefit of the persuaded, benefit for the persuader and the persuaded or mutual benefit for the persuaded individual and a third party. All these results have a positive result for the person to be convinced. Sometimes other people benefit, sometimes they don't. However, there is no situation where only the manipulator benefits.

Dark persuasion has a very distinct set of results. The persuader always advantages either immediately or by his distorted need for control and impact. The persuaded individual is against their own self-interest and is not persuaded. Finally, not only do the most qualified dark persuaders' damage their victims, but they also damage others. Take a dark persuader who tells somebody to commit suicide so they can take advantage of an insurance policy. The persuader not only won financially, but also the victim lost his life and hurt everyone who knew or cared for them.

Who are these individuals who often tend to use dark persuasion? The main characteristic of a dark persuader is either indifference or an inability to be concerned about the impact of persuasion on others. They are either completely narcissistic and regard their own requirements to be far more essential than the requirements of others or they are sociopathic and unable to even understand the notion of the feelings of others. In a partnership, you often discover dark persuasion. In the worst case scenario, both partners are inclined to persuade the other darkly. The connection can be regarded psychologically abusive if such efforts are persistent and durable. Some instances of dark relationships include not allowing the other partner to take fresh jobs or to take private pleasure. The obscure persuader will persuade the victim to act "for the sake of friendship." The victim merely hurts himself and the relationship in fact. The connection is being damaged as the dark persuader gains greater assurance that his victims can be manipulated.

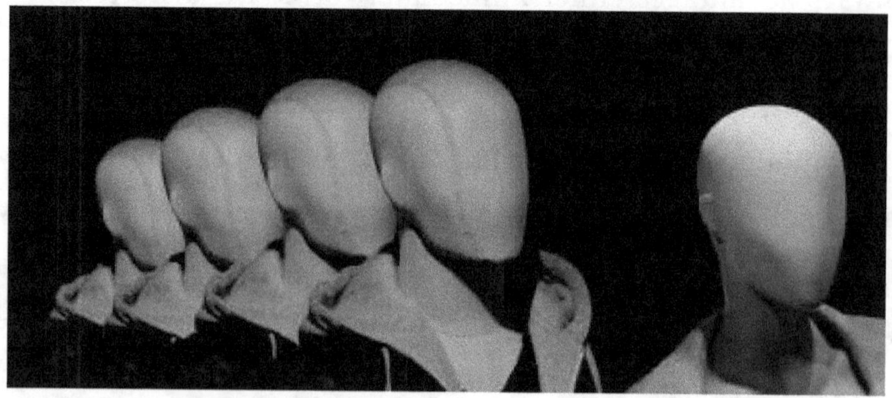

Elements of persuasion

Like other types of control, some components are to be observed when it comes to persuasion. These components assist to precisely identify which persuasion makes it clearer. The ability to convince others is one salient feature that distinguishes persuasion from all other themes of dark psychology since the victim is in most cases allowed to make choices out of their own will, I as much as persuasion tactics will later work towards changing his will to that of the persuader. The topic can choose the manner they want to believe, whether or not they want to buy a product, or whether they believe the proof behind the persuasion is powerful enough to alter their minds. There are a few components in persuasion that assist to further describe what is while giving us a deeper understanding of this enigmatic theme.

The first element of this theme is that persuasion is often symbolic. What this means is that persuasion utilizes words, sound as well as images so as to get the message across to the specific victim. The logic behind this is quite simple really. For one individual to be able to persuade another into acting in a particular way, they will need to show them why they should act in said way and not vice versa. This is best achieved by using word sounds or various images you can use sentences to start a debate or argument to prove your point. Pictures are a great way to show the evidence needed to persuade someone to go one way or the other. Some nonverbal signs are possible, but they are not as effective as using words and images

The second key is that persuasion will be used deliberately to affect how others act or think. This one is quite obvious; you don't use persuasion to get them to change if you don't deliberately try to affect others. In order to get the topic to believe the same way they do, the persuader will attempt distinct strategies. This could be as easy as having a discussion with them or presenting proof supporting their point of perspective. On the other hand, to change the mind of the subject, it could involve much more and include more deceptive forms.

The distinctive thing about persuasion is that it enables some type of free will for the topic. In this way, the topic is permitted to create its own decision. For the most part, they don't have to go for it, no matter how hard somebody tries to persuade them of something. The subject might hear about the best car to buy a thousand commercials, but if they don't like that brand or don't need a new vehicle at that time, they won't go out and buy it. If the subject is against abortion, how many people will come out and say how great abortion is, it's not likely that the subject will change their minds This enables much more freedom of choice than is found in the other types of mind control, which could explain why when questioned, many individuals do not see this as a kind of mind control. Persuasion is a type of mind control that can take place in many respects. While brainwashing, hypnosis and manipulation must happen face-to-face, and in some instances in full isolation, persuasion may happen otherwise.

Examples of persuasion can be found everywhere, including when you talk to individuals you know, on the Internet, on radio and television. It is also feasible to deliver persuasive messages by nonverbal and verbal means; although when verbal methods are used it is much more efficient

Subliminal persuasion

The word "subliminal" means underneath our consciousness. Subliminal persuasion means an advertising message that is displayed below the threshold of awareness or consumer awareness in order to persuade, persuade or help people change their minds without making them aware of what is going on. This is about affecting individuals with more than words. Some of the subliminal methods of persuasion impact our stimuli with smell, eyesight, sound, touch, and taste. There are mainly 3 subliminal methods of persuasion to affect anyone. They are

- Building a relationship-building relationship makes the other person feel comfortable. This will open up the other individual more. This can be accomplished through a healthy observation strength that matches their mood or state. This helps create confidence

- Power of discussion—the power of a powerful convincing person is much connected to an advertiser's conversion. The correct words and inflections help you to be openly straightforward.

- Suggestive power-Associating useful and desirable stuff in discussion or interaction enables an individual to become more open to fresh thoughts.

Suggestion and emotional intelligence

This stage may be described as having one central and dominant idea focused on the participant's conscious mind, which was to stimulate or decrease the physiological performance of the various regions within the participant's body. Later on, the use of different non-verbal and verbal suggestions was increasingly emphasized in order to convince the participant easily.

Basic Persuasion techniques

There are techniques that can be utilized so as to make persuasion more successful. All victims are usually presented with different forms of persuasion on a daily basis. A food manufacturing plant will work on getting their victims to purchase a new product, while a movie company will focus on persuading their victims to watch their latest movie projects. There are three main techniques of persuasion that have been prevalent since the birth of this theme.

Create a need

This is one of the techniques that are often deployed by the manipulator so as to be able to get the victim to change their way of thinking. This creates a need or rather appeals to a need that is already pre-existing within the victim. If it is executed in a skilled way, the victim will be eating out of the persuader's palm in no time. What this means is that the manipulator will need to tap into the fundamental needs of their victim like for example their need for self-actualization. This technique will in most casework so well for the manipulator because the victim is actually going to need these things. Food for example is usually something that we as humans need in order to survive and prolonged lack will pause as a big problem. If the agent can convince the subject that their store is the best, or if they can get more food or shelter by switching their beliefs, there is a higher chance of success.

Utilizing illustrative and words

The choice of words one chooses to use comes a long way in the success of using persuasion. There are many ways in which you can phrase sentences when actually talking about one thing. Saying the right words in the right way is what will make all the difference when attempting to use persuasion.

Tricks used by mass media and advertising

The media use two main methods which they use to persuade the masses. First is through the use of images, as well as the use of sounds.

Media persuasion by use of images

Our sighs and visual processing areas of the brain are very powerful. Just think about it for a minute, have you ever thought of a person without ending up picturing how they look? It is because of this that makes imagery and visual manipulation a preferred method by the media. Companies will often include split-second images of their product or individual inserted into an advertisement that seems quite innocent on the face value. This usually a form of subliminal persuasion. These split-second images that are usually assumed for the most part usually end up taking some form of control of the victim, which persuades them to purchase that particular service.

Media persuasion by the use of sound

Sound is yet another trick that is used by media in the persuasion of unsuspecting victims. Some people usually underestimate the powers that exist within the sound. But answer me this, how many times have you heard a song somewhere only to have it loops through your mind continuously? Songs usually have an influence on us even though we are not aware of it despite knowing you are listening to it. This is what the media tend to exploit in their quest for persuasion of the masses. There will often be a number of phrases skillfully hidden, and repeated in an advertisement song that will most likely convince you to be inclined to prefer one company over the other. An example of this is seen at McDonald's. The melody 'I'm lovin it 'is often repeated in a manner that persuades the victims to constantly purchase their meals.

Chapter 2 Advanced Persuasion Techniques

Dark Persuasion Techniques to Be on the Lookout For

After taking a look at the different types of persuasion and what they all mean, you may be able to see why dark persuasion is such a bad thing and can be harmful to the victim. Being able to recognize the different techniques that the manipulator may use can make it easier to understand when it is being used on you.

So, how exactly is a dark persuader able to use this idea in order to carry out their wishes? There are a few different types of tactics that a dark manipulator is going to use, but some of the most common options include:

The Long Con

The first method that we are going to look at is the Long Con. This method is kind of slow and drawn out, but it can be really effective because it takes so long and is hard to recognize or even pinpoint when something went wrong. One of the main reasons that some people have the ability to resist persuasion is because they feel that they are being pressured by the other person, and this can make them back off. If they feel that there is a lack of rapport or trust with the person who is trying to persuade them, they will steer clear as well. The Long Con is so effective because they are able to overcome these main problems and give the persuader exactly what they want.

The Long Con is going to involve the dark persuader to take their time, working to earn the trust of their victim. They are going to take some time to befriend the victim and make sure that their victim trusts and likes them. This is going to be achieved by the persuader with artificial rapport building, which sometimes seems excessive, and other techniques that will help to increase the comfort levels between the persuader and their victim.

As soon as the persuader sees that the victim is properly readied psychologically, the persuader is going to begin their attempts. It starts in slow successions of convincing the individual then the victim manages to do as the persuader wants. This is going to serve the persuader in two ways. First, the victim starts to become used to persuasion by that persuader. The second is that the victim is going to start making that mental association between a positive outcome and the persuasion.

The Long Con is going to take a long period of time to complete because the persuader doesn't want to make it too obvious what they are doing. An example of this is a victim who is a recently widowed lady who is vulnerable because of her age and from their bereavement. After her loss, a man starts to befriend her. This man may be someone she knows from church or even a relative. He starts to spend more time with her, showing immense kindness and patience, and it doesn't take too long for her guard to drop when he comes around.

Then this man starts to carry out some smaller acts of positive persuasion that we talked about before. He may advise her of a better bank account to use or a better way to reduce any monthly bills. The victim is going to appreciate these efforts and the fact that the man is trying to help her, and she takes the advice.

Over some time, the man then tries to use some dark persuasion. He may try to persuade her to let him invest some of her money. She obliges because of the positive persuasion that was used in the past. Of course, the man is going to work to take everything he can get from her. If the manipulator is skilled enough, she may feel that he actually tried to help her, but the money is lost because he just ran into some bad luck with the investment. This is how far dark persuasion can go.

Graduality

Often when we hear about acts of dark persuasion, it seems impossible and unbelievable. What they fail to realize is that this dark persuasion isn't ever going to be a big or a sudden request that comes out of nowhere. Dark persuasion is more like a staircase. The dark persuader is never going to ask the victim to do something big and dramatic the first time they meet. Instead, they will have the victim take one step at a time.

When the manipulator has the target only go one step at a time, the whole process seems like less of a big deal. Before the victim knows it, they have already gone a long way down, and the persuader isn't likely to let them leave or come back up again.

Let's take an example of how this process is going to look in real life. Let's say that there is a criminal who wanted to make it so that someone else committed the crimes for them. Gang bosses, cult leaders, and even Charles Manson did this exact same thing.

This criminal wouldn't dream of beginning the process by asking their victim to murder for them. This would send out a red flag, and no one in their right minds would willingly go out and kill for someone they barely know. Instead, the criminal would start out by having the victim do something small, like a petty crime, or simply hiding a weapon for them. Something that isn't that big of a deal for the victim, at least in comparison.

Over time, the acts that the manipulator is able to persuade their victim to do will become more severe. And since they did the smaller crimes, the persuader passes such actions to the victim (blackmailing). Before the victim knows it, they are going to feel like they are in too deep. They will then be persuaded to carry out some of the most shocking crimes. And often, by this point, they will do it because they feel like they have no other choice.

Dark persuaders are going to be experts at using this graduality to help increase the severity of their persuasion over time. They know that no victim would be willing to jump the canyon or do the big crime or misdeed right away. So, the persuader works to build a bridge to get there. By the time the victim sees how far in they are, it is too late to turn back.

Masking the True Intentions

There are different methods that a persuader is able to use dark psychology in order to get the things that they want. Disguising their true desires is very important for them to be successful. The best persuaders can use this approach in a variety of ways, but the method they choose is often going to depend on the victim and the situation.

One principle that is used by a persuader is the idea that many people are going to have a difficult time refusing two requests when they happen in a row. Let's say that the persuader wants to get $200 from the victim, but they do not intend to repay the money. To start, the persuader may begin by saying that they need a loan for the amount of $1000. They may go into some details about the consequences to themselves if the persuader doesn't come up with that kind of money sometime soon.

It may happen that the victim feels some kind of guilt or compassion to the persuader, and they want to help. But $1000 is a lot of money, more than the victim is able to lend. From here, the persuader is going to lessen their request from $1000 down to $200, the amount that they wanted from the beginning. Of course, there is some kind of emotional reason for needing the money, and the victim feels like it is impossible to refuse this second request. They want to help out the persuader, and they feel bad for not giving in to the initial request when they were asked. In the end, the persuader gets the $200 they originally wanted, and the victim is not going to know what has taken place.

Another type of technique that the persuader can use is known as reverse psychology. This can also help to mask the true intentions during the persuasion. Some people have a personality that is known as a boomerang. This means that they will refuse to go in the direction that they are thrown and instead will veer off into different directions.

If the persuader knows someone who is more of a boomerang type, then they are able to identify a key weakness of that person. For example, let's say that a persuader has a friend who is attempting to win over some girl they like. The persuader knows that the friend will use and then hurt that girl. The girl is currently torn between the malicious friend and an innocent third party. The persuader may try to steer the girl in the direction of the guy who is actually a good choice, knowing that she is going to go against this and end up going with the harmful friend.

Leading Questions

Another method of dark persuasion that can be used is known as leading questions. If you have ever had an encounter with a salesman that is skilled, verbal persuasion can be really impactful when it is deployed in careful and calibrated ways. One of the most powerful techniques that can be used verbally is leading questions.

These leading questions are going to be any questions that are intended to trigger a specific response out of the victim. The persuader may ask the target something like "how bad do you think those people are?" This question is going to imply that the people the persuader is asking about are definitely bad to some extent. They could have chosen to ask a question that was non-leading, such as "how do you feel about those people?"

Dark persuaders are masters at using leading questions in a way that is hard to catch. If the victim ever begins to feel that they are being led, then they are going to resist, and it is hard to lead them or persuade them. If a persuader ever senses that their victim starts to catch what is happening, they will quit using that one and switch over to another one. They may come back to that tactic, but only when the victim has quieted down a bit and is more influenceable again.

The Law of State Transference

State is a concept that is going to take a look at the general mood someone is in. If someone is aligned with their deeds, words, and thoughts, then this is an example of a strong and congruent state. The law of state transference is going to involve the concept of someone who holds the balance of power in a situation and can then transfer their emotional state onto the other person they are interacting with. This can be a very powerful tool for the dark persuader to use against their victim.

Initially, the influencer is going to force their own state to match the state that their target naturally has. If the target is sad, and they talk slowly, the influencer is going to make their own state follow this format. The point of this is to create a deep rapport with the target.

After we get to this state match, the influencer is then going to alter their own state subtly and see if they have some compliance for the victim. Perhaps they will choose to speed up their own voice to see if the victim will speed up as well. Once the victim starts to show these signs of compliance, then this is an indication that the influencer is at the hook point.

As soon as this hook point is reached, though it may take some time depending on the target and the situation, then the influencer is going to change their own personal state to the one they want the victim to have. This could be any emotional state that the influencer wants. It could be positive, angry, happy, or indignant. It often depends on what the persuader wants to help reach their goals. This technique is an important one for a dark persuader because it is going to show the impact of subconscious cues on the failure or the success of any type of persuasion.

Chapter 3 Difference Between Persuasion And Manipulation

Truly, these two concepts are very closely related and most of the people get confused between their differences and meanings and the line between them seems blurred. It is crucial for you to figure out when you are crossing the line of persuasion and entering into manipulation zone. Hence, before understanding what is the difference in them, let us first understand the meaning of them which would clear out the difference automatically.

Persuasion means when you say or act in such a way that people do or believe what you are saying. Persuasion is something that we do every day on a daily basis. Persuasion is never taken in evil or negative way. We can say that it is the way we interact with the people who are around us. At times while discussing any topic when we try to keep our point and prove ourselves right, that as well is persuasion. It also comes in picture when you want someone to do something right and want to see this world as a better place. Also, at times you try to persuade people when you want to earn a profit or sell a product and doing this is not being wicked or doing something immoral.

Let us understand this by taking an example when you make a product according to the customer's needs and requirements and want to make the journey of the buyer easy and then you are trying to convince them to buy it as you know it will benefit them and you both.

Now, let us understand what manipulation means. It means the act to change by unfair or artful means to serve your purpose. In manipulation, you are not bothered about the other person's benefit or less what you want to see is your revenue and benefit. In this case, you want your profit no matter what, by any means. If in case the buyer as well is benefiting then that is good but they are not concerned about that. Manipulation always comprises of deception and misrepresentation of the product or truth, but it does not go a long way.

Let us understand this as well by taking an example in relevance to the above-mentioned one. Here the company thinks of only their profit while making the profit irrespective of thinking about the customer needs and requirements. In such cases, the customer would only try the product once and when they will realize that it is not helping them or they have been deceived they would stop buying the product.

Most of the researchers say that the difference between the two comes down to basically three things which are-

a) The intention behind your persuasion

b) Transparency and truthfulness behind your desire

c) A benefit to the other person

- These were the major differences between persuasion and manipulation. Yes, there is a very thin line of intention between them, but it is important for you to realize it. Persuasion is always positive and manipulations are said to be negative and evil. With the help of persuasion in an argument, you try to make the interlocutor adopt your point of view, on the other hand, in manipulation; you bent the truth to get approval from the interlocutor. In persuasion, the opponent willing accepts your point but in manipulation, the person is coerced to agree.

- Persuasion is usually done with the intention to do good things. Here you would try to recommend the buyer with the best services and try to make the perfect match and also would strive that the person stops using anything which is harmful. On the contrary in manipulation, only one of the parties is benefited

- In persuasion, you present all the right arguments in the best manner which are logical and convincing both but in manipulation people try to mould the truth so that they can achieve their selfish goals

- Although, in persuasion as well you try to convince others when they do not agree to your point. But the thing is that you are being transparent and the intentions are good and real. On the other hand, manipulation is opposite

- In persuasion, if the other person agrees to what you were trying to tell they would benefit by it as it was in their favor. But in manipulation, the other person would regret after agreeing to your point. The reason behind it is that the truth was not told, the customer had no benefit as the intent was never good.

I am sure by now it must be very clear to you that what does both these things mean and what are the major differences in them. Therefore, you should always think while convincing someone that does it benefit just you or the other person as well. It will become easy for you to understand whether you are doing something wrong or are you right.

Don't you think persuasion is a really good technique and every one of us should imply it in our lives and think about ours and others benefits too? So, let us learn a few persuasion tactics which would help you in changing other's mind-

- Scarcity Technique- This is the most used persuasion technique and mostly the salesman and marketers use it. I am sure that you must have seen that the product which is less in supply, people tend to ask more of it. Thus, if you want to increase the demand of your product or service always show that it is available for a limited time or the offer is just for the

time being, it would increase the chances of increase in sales of your product. You must have read these lines many times such as never to be seen again, once a year, attaching a timer, limited offer, etc. Also, there was an experiment done where one group was given a product which was in great amount and the other group was given a product which was scarce. The end of this experiment was the second group could sell more products as people were keen to buy it because it was limited. You as well can use this tactic to increase the demand for your commodities.

- Social Authentication- People usually consider this technique as it does not take time to notice that in social groups people usually there are group thinkers of higher level. Whenever anyone thinks of a unique idea whatever everyone agrees or not but yes they think and give their point of view. So, whenever you will take any decision, in that regard you will always consider the points that your mates or friends mentioned. For example, there are many people who just start smoking either because for them it is social proof or their friends too so they also start doing it.

- Reciprocation- Most of the people like returning favors if someone does something good for them. Also, majorly people do not even know that they would like the gift or not they are just inclined to return the favor back. If you make someone feel indebted that is a good way increases the probability of getting what you desire. For example, you want to collect money for some old age people so that they can get a house. Instead of directly asking for money, according to their talent, you can ask them to make beautiful frames, pots, etc. Give them to people, make them feel indebted and then ask for a donation. Also, a study was done and seen the more kind the waiter was with the customers the more tip he got. So, be generous to all and they would in turn return generosity towards you.

- Authority- If you want to convince people always to show yourself as a source of authority. As most people look up to authority or a leader be it any field and get easily convinced when an authoritative person says something. For example, if you read that 9 out of 10 doctors recommend using a specific brand of soap, then most of the people would run after that brand as it has gained an advantage over others. This states that the majority of the people follow someone who has authority, at times even when they are wrong. This technique explains to you that always be confident and have your own attitude if you want people to follow you or get influenced by what you say or do.

- Regularity and commitment- It has been seen that people who show regularity and fulfill the promises then it helps them in influencing others to do more for them. Such as if you fulfill the commitment and do what you said in time, it influences others and make them believe that they can count on you and can help you in persuasion when you want them to do something for you. For example, many websites instead of writing signup, use the statement like- join me and the second option is No, I am boring. Statements like this convince customers and it increases their conversion rates.

- Foot in the door- This persuasion technique is very interesting and many people use it. This technique states that whenever you want a favor from someone, first ask for a smaller one and then ask for the bigger favor. It means that when you first ask for help and if the person says yes, they get committed to doing that and when you ask for the bigger help it can act as a continuation for the smaller one. For example, if you fail in a test and your teacher says no for taking the test again. You should first always ask for the feedback so that you can work on it. And then request the teacher whether they can take the test again. This way the teacher would see that you are really keen to learn and improve and would not say no.

- Door in the Face- Well, this technique has been seen in many stores and supermarkets. It is the opposite of the technique mentioned above. In this method, you first ask for big favors and if the person says no then request and ask if they can do something easy and small for you. This way the other person gets convinced and thinks that if not a big help but yes then can do a favor by doing something small. For example, you ask your cousin or any mate for Rs.10,000 if they say no then you can always say that if not 10,000 can you please help me with Rs. 3000? There are major possibilities that they would say yes.

- Anchoring- This is said to one of the most powerful persuasion methods. It has numerous uses but is mostly used in pricing. This technique can be best explained with the help of an example. You go to the market to buy a refrigerator for yourself, the salesman says Rs. 30,999 but you bargain and get the cost lowered to Rs.27,500. You would be happy that you got a great deal and feel satisfied, instead of knowing that the actual price of it was maybe less than that. But you are happy as according to you it was the best deal.

These were the best persuasion techniques which you can apply to your daily life if required as they are not manipulative but are very convincing and can also get your work done easily and quickly.

It is also prime for us to know some of the manipulator's emotional techniques and how to deal with them as they might be very difficult for you to point out if you are not aware of-

- No point coming in their words- Manipulators are wise enough to turn the statements that you say. Whatever you would say, they have explanations for everything and would turn the things around. For example, if they forget any special occasion and you complain them for it, they would always have explanation such as I am so sorry, I did not want to spoil your mood but I am having a bad time at my work and was very much busy in it. If you think and it seems as the apology is fake, make sure that you do not come in their words. In such cases, always trust your intuition and if you feel it is fake, then do not accept the apology. Once you agree to it, then you will always be treated the same way.

- They pretend well that they want to help you- They are very good at faking out that they want to help you. They would at first say yes but make expressions that will show you that they are not willing to help you. And when you ask them if they do not want to help, then they would always pretend and say of course I want to help you and say how unreasonable you are.

Ensure that if a manipulator says yes, held them accountable for it, do not buy their reasons. Make sure that if they do not want to do it they say it upfront, instead of saying yes to be in the good books.

- Dirty Fights- The worst part about them is that they would not fight directly with you, instead they would bitch around your back and ask others to convey the message as they would not want to deal with it directly. They would find different ways to let you know that they are not happy with you or not talking to you. First, they would show that they support you, but at the time of help, they would act weirdly. Such as they would ask you to study further and say that they support you but when you have exams they will call their friends for a house party. And when you fight with them on this they would have answers like life cannot stop, I have a life too. So make sure you make decisions on your own without being dependent as it can come back to you in a wicked manner.

- The impact the environment around them- They are so selfish that they just care about themselves and nothing else matters to them. When they are angry or do not get something that they wish for, they would change the climate around. The only way to fix it is to give them what they want to make them happy. But be careful, these people would let you forget your own needs and keep you busy with their requirements always. If you are with someone like this take a step back or think about the relationship again.

These kinds of behaviors are difficult to handle and escape, so be brave and bold if you are around people who are manipulators and take a step. Either face them or just ignore them, do not stay with them.

Dark Persuasion and Covert Manipulation

As you have understood the concept of persuasion and manipulation in the above section, now it's time to know some other aspects of them which are Dark persuasion and covert manipulation. As in the above paragraphs, you have clearly understood what persuasion is. The difference between dark persuasion and persuasion is of intentions. A persuader always tries to convince through particular techniques or motivation without having any sort of understanding about the person whom they are trying to convince. He is only concerned about doing good for people and thinking of their benefit along with their own. He does everything with a good intention without too many facts and figures of the person whom they are trying to convince.

On the other hand, dark persuader also thinks and analyzes a bigger picture. They very well understand that what are the tactics they need to use to succeed and how far do they need to take it. They only think that they are doing something right but are unconcerned with the morality of manipulation he does. They always try to achieve whatever they want through any means whichever the feel can be more effective.

Persuasion is never without moral implications but in dark persuasion moral implications are just not the determining factor. There are many other factors which are more important than being morally correct. The smartest thing about a dark persuader is that in their circle they would be the most selfish person but would show and seem that they are least selfish. They would get exactly what they get, without the other person knowing or even realizing.

The other thing that a dark persuader does is knowing about the weakness of others. This helps them in extracting words, presents, and gifts which they can take or give according to their advantage and situation. For example, if an employer knows that he has illegal immigrants working in his company, he can always lower his wages as per his choice as they know that they cannot work anywhere else in the country.

Dark persuasion can vary from small to very large scale, such as a kid asking his elder brother for all the ice cream he has to a leader trying to ask for help in war to defeat another country. So, to determine dark persuasion it is always vital to understand the different personalities and their circumstances.

Covert manipulation is even worse than manipulation, in this, the manipulator tries to use the emotional vulnerability to their benefit. They would strive to their best so that they can know about your goals, strengths, weaknesses, fear, family, etc. So that they can use all of these factors to make you feel low and weak. It is said to be underhanded methods of control. It operates under your level of conscious awareness. The bad part of it is that the victim is not even aware that they are being manipulated, that is the reason it becomes prime for you to know about the manipulation games that these people use.

Covert manipulation is very dangerous as it is so subtle and underhanded that it takes a long time before you can make out that you were being manipulated. According to research, it was also found that there are few manipulators with such sharp skills that they are called puppet masters, you would without even knowing become their puppets, so it is important for you to know their signs so that you can take the actions accordingly. They would make you feel that you are doing according to your own wish but the truth is that you do that only what they ask you to do.

Sometimes you might feel that something is wrong but you would not be able to analyze that someone is trying to manipulate you. In covert manipulation first thing which is prime is that you should ask yourself if you are being manipulated? As covert manipulation is adverse and has a negative effect on us, so it would be easier for you to understand that you are being manipulated.

It is significant for you to understand a few characteristics of a covert manipulator, so it becomes really easy for you to spot them if they are around you-

1) Lying- They would lie straight in your eyes and you would not even get to know that they are lying. They would tell you twisted truth or half-truth which you might or might not get to know later. If you ever have any doubts on the other person about the truth, you should always double-check the information so that it does not hamper your relationship or work.

2) Backhanded compliments- This is something they are best at. Covert manipulators are great in giving backhanded compliments. They would give compliments as you did it in a great way although you are so weak and low in confidence, still, you handled it well. You cooked so well, although you do not cook for me often. These compliments make you feel even more embarrassed and awkward, where you do not even know how to react. In such cases, the best thing is to ignore or giving them the taste of their own medicine by replying in the same way.

3) Mirroring- The coincidences would be extravagant. They would agree to all your points, likes, dislikes, taste, color, etc just to impress you or to be with you. When they want to take benefit from you they would agree to all your things and choices. Once they get what they wanted everything would change. You would feel that the person has fully switched. So, you should always beware of the person who agrees to whatever you say without

keeping their point of you, it straight away means that they are trying to be manipulative.

4) Rationalization- This is something many people would do to cover their lies or fault. They would cook new stories to cover their flaws such as the reason why you did not tell that you had a girlfriend before me, the reason they would give you would be like I did not want to lose you by telling this or I did not know how you would react after listening to this, etc. Thu they would have answers for all the lies, so make sure that you know and follow your gut feel to analyze if he is saying right or just faking it.

5) Hurried Intimacy- This is a very alarming sign of a covert manipulator. They would very quickly tell you about their goals, achievements, passion and past and what ask you the same things. Once you open up with them, they would use this information to control and manipulate you. Therefore, you should always be wise enough to understand when to share the information and how much information to share. They would be very quick in proposing for marriage and talking about the future but you need to be careful before telling your weaknesses.

6) Playing the victim- This is another thing they do to gain your sympathy. Just to gain your love and attention they would lie to you to any extent. They might say that their childhood was very bad as the parents were not good, etc. Just to get more love and care from you. They might make any stories for your love and

care, so always know the past first before you get so much involved.

7) Silent Treatment- Leaving room or house for a couple of hours, would not engage in any activity, etc. They also hide behaviors or start avoiding you so that you realize it is your mistake or you start the conversation. They keep the concerns unspoken within them which is a dangerous sign too.

8) Belittling- They do react weird such as rolling the eyes, scoffing, mocking, teasing, etc. They do not even respect others point of view or abilities, and they always want another person to feel low and always try to demean them. You should always maintain a distance with such covert people who are jealous of your success and feel bad seeing you rise.

9) Word Play- A covert manipulator very well knows what you want to hear and would please your ears by saying that. They know how to put a convincing statement, paint the picture well and also to induce an emotional reaction in front of you. Not only this, they are great it talking double meaning things, they would mean something else but say it in a different context. For example, please marry me I will change your life. This can be in any aspect positive or negative. So be precise and clear while talking to a covert manipulator.

10) Finance controller- Covet manipulator not only restrict by playing with your emotions they are also good in controlling and gaming with your finances too. For example, accessing your

account but denying access to their account, taking things on loan in joint names without even asking you, running up debts, borrowing and not paying, etc. These are very tricky things which you should be careful about and take a step in time before they make your account nil.

These were the few characteristics of a covert manipulator which you should be diligent about so that nobody can take advantage of you or humiliate you.

Chapter 4 The Psychology Of Persuasion

The Power Of Persuasion

The power of persuasion means nothing more than using mental abilities to form words and feelings used to convince other people to do things they may or may not want to do. Some people are better able to persuade than other people. And some people are easier to persuade then other people.

The ease of persuading other people is directly tied to their current mental or emotional state. Someone who is lonely or tired is easier to persuade, simply because their defenses are lowered. Someone who is momentarily needy may be easier to persuade than someone who has a strong sense of self-worth. People who are at a low point in their lives are easy prey for others who might try to persuade them to do something they might not usually do.

The first step in persuasion involves the idea of reciprocating. If a person does something nice for someone else, then the receiving person usually feels the need to do something good in return. If someone helps their elderly neighbor carry in groceries from the car, that neighbor might feel obligated to bake homemade cookies for that person. A coworker who helps complete a project is more likely to receive assistance when it is needed. Many people do nice things for others all the time without expecting anything in return. The person who does nice things for people and then mentions some little favor that can be done in return may be someone to watch closely.

Nonprofit organizations use this tactic to gain more contributions to their causes. They will often send some little trinket or gift to prompt people to donate larger sums of money, or even just to donate where they might not have originally. The idea behind this is that the person opening the letter has received a little gift for no reason, so they might feel obligated to give something in return.

Some people are automatically tempted to follow authority. People in positions of authority can command blind respect to their authority simply by acting a certain way or putting on a uniform. The problem with this is that authority figures or those that look like authority figures, can cause some people to do extraordinary things they would not normally do had a person in a position of authority not been the one asking. And it is not simply held to people in uniform. People who carry themselves a certain way or speak a certain way can give the impression that they are something they are not.

For someone or something to be considered a credible authority, it must be familiar and people must have trust in the person or organization. Someone who knows all there is to know about a subject is considered an expert and is more likely to be trusted than someone who has limited knowledge of the subject. But the information must also make sense to the people hearing it. If there is not some semblance of accuracy and intelligence, then the authority figure loses credibility. Even the person who is acknowledged as an expert will lack persuasive abilities if they are seen as not being trustworthy.

The worst part of the power that goes along with persuasion is that things that are scarce or hard to get are seen as much more valuable. People value diamonds because they are expensive and beautiful. If they were merely pretty stones, they would not be as interesting. Inconsistent rewards are a lot more interesting than consistent rewards. If a cookie falls every time a person rings a bell, then they are less likely to spend a lot of time ringing the bell because they know the cookie reward will always appear. If, however, the cookie only appears sometimes, people will spend much more time ringing the bell just in case this is the time the cookie will fall.

There are ways to improve the power of persuasion. Just like any other trait, it can be made stronger by following a few strategies and by regular practice.

Persuasion is a powerful tool in the game of life. Persuasive people know that they have an amazing power, and they know how to use it correctly. They know how to listen and really hear what other people have to say. They are very good at making a connection with other people, and this makes them seem even more honest and friendly. They make others feel that they are knowledgeable and can offer a certain sense of satisfaction. They also know when to momentarily retreat and regroup. They are not pushy. They are persuasive.

Did you know that your body speaks more eloquently than words? Body language is at work constantly whether you are aware of it or not. When you want to master the art of persuasion, you need not only understand (and read accurately) body language, but also learn to use it to drive your point home.

Body language is a mix of hand and facial gestures, posture and overall appearance. Using these to your advantage you can get people to do what you want without them realizing that you are actually controlling the outcome of the discussion.

Why people are persuasive

What makes a person convincing? Why are they persuasive, and you aren't? This is the answer we're going to pursue in this e-book, but I'm telling you now, there is no single, short answer to that question.

What makes this persuasive influence so difficult to pin down and elusive is precisely this almost mosaic quality it has. It's the result, the perfect merger of several important aspects that you wouldn't normally attribute to such an influence.

These aspects of their being don't only affect them, but affect us, as well. That's the fascination around it. It's all psychological, it's an overwhelming and sometimes unintentional psychological influence on the people around them.

Confidence is the absolute most important aspect when it comes to persuasion. There's no doubt it's been scientifically proven that it's easier to persuade people when you're confident. That's because it's just assumed you're an authority on the topic and they'll listen to you, because they have no knowledge or experience, but you seem to have both.

It's also crucial to understand that humans are doubtful creatures. We're not very confident and we don't really believe in our own abilities or even experience, so when someone comes along and appears to be confident and to know more, we follow them like a herd of dim sheep.

Persuasion is just as much about the impression you leave upon people as it is about your actual skill. Like many other times in life, appearances are more "real" than actual reality, because it's all other people will ever know about you. It doesn't matter if deep inside, you're insecure or you don't really think you know what you're doing.

On the outside, you're this dazzling, confident creature that can persuade anyone into anything because you've mastered all the important contributing factors: confidence, eye contact, body language, manner of speaking, tone, facial expressions, as well as your general demeanor.

Confidence

How do you think so many scammers make a living? No, that sketchy guy selling you snake oil isn't really a doctor, but he speaks like he is one, so people believe him and throw money at him, genuinely believing he will solve their problems.

Now, I'm not advocating that you try to trick people, but I am telling you that you need to work on your confidence. You'll notice that every single person you find convincing has some sort of authoritative stance. It's like their presence demands attention and respect.

Eye contact

Eye contact is a classic, natural display of dominance. It's a technique that's even present in the animal kingdom, and if a lion doesn't intimidate you, I don't know who can. It's true that the goal isn't to intimidate? Eye contact can do that very effectively.

Body language

Do you know how often people underestimate body language, or just ignore it outright? I don't know why, because body language is an amazing tool for persuasion. People are always advised to display open body language, like facing your audience, making sure not to keep your arms crossed against your chest, keep your palms open, and all sorts of little tips that we'll discuss at length later.

What you maybe haven't heard is that in order to be effectively persuasive, you also need to take note of and use the body language of the person you're talking to.

Manner of speaking

Your choice of words is overwhelmingly important when attempting to convince someone, because it must be very deliberate. There's a clear strategy behind verbal persuasion, and it relies on appealing to the person's emotions.

The way you speak and what you say are both equally important, because even though your message may be perfect, if the delivery is lacking, it won't do much good. We've already established that speaking with authority is half the battle, but you also have to speak the right words, in order to win it.

Tone

Continuing on the idea that the way you say things is vastly important, let's talk about tone and why it matters. In fact, I lied when I said tone and message are equally important: tone weighs much more on a person's impression.

If someone has a very somber voice, a serious, measured tone, and an equally severe facial expression, it almost doesn't matter what they're saying – you're going to assume it's grave and important; the actual words or what they mean matters less. A joke told with a serious tone isn't funny at all.

Facial expressions

Facial expression goes hand in hand with body language and eye contact and is similarly important to tonality. Creating the impression that you mean what you say involves your face, because it will be the very first to betray you or, on the contrary, help you enforce your message.

What you can obtain through persuasion

Persuasion is a very powerful and very valuable skill that not everyone has, but that everyone should have. It comes in handy throughout your life in virtually any aspect of your existence, from sweet-talking your way into free movie tickets to convincing your boss you deserve a raise.

Your relationship with your spouse

Far from being unfair or manipulative, having the ability to convince your significant other can actually improve your relationship because you have fewer fights about your disagreements and lack of compromise. Now you can use all that extra time and energy implementing your superior decisions.

Your relationship with your kids

Having the persuasion skills and indisputable power and authority to convince your kids to actually do what you tell them to is as close to magic as you can possibly get. If you don't believe me, try it!

Your relationship with your friends

We all have that one friend who always makes terrible life choices and no one can get through to them and steer them towards the right path...except you, that is. If you have influence and persuasion skills, don't keep them for yourself. Use them for good, not evil.

Get paid what you deserve

Negotiating absolutely falls under persuasion, so really, absolutely everyone should have this skill. No matter if you're haggling at the market or discussing a higher salary, you need to have the ability to convince your 'opponent' that you deserve this and you should have it.

It's mostly applicable in the workplace, where – let's be real – no boss will ever willingly part with their money and hand it over to you. So it's your job to convince them to do it. You've earned it, you deserve it, and it's rightfully yours. You have to ask for it, but you have to know how, and persuasive skills help with that.

Earn the trust and respect of your boss

You can accomplish that by becoming their go-to person. Offer your bright ideas, come up with solutions to problems the company is facing, persuade them to implement your suggestions and that they're the contribution the company needs right now. In time, you will reap the rewards when your boss comes to consult with your first.

Be a good leader to your colleagues

Obviously, your persuasive abilities will prove to be invaluable to a position like this if you want people to respect you, your work, and your ideas. It should be obvious for everyone that your way is the right way and there will be minimal dissent if you have the necessary influence over them.

Get out of paying tickets

Legally, a ticket is a mandatory consequence of breaking the law in some way, by speeding, failing to wear your seatbelt, talking on your cell while driving, *etc.* Practically, however…a ticket can be a negotiation, as long as you have the necessary skills.

Get into coveted clubs or restaurants

If you're persuasive enough, you can influence any menial gatekeeper and convince them to just let you through without needing to jump through fiery hoops or grease the well-meaning palms of anyone. Talk about some sweet perks!

Get important information

If you can talk the talk well enough, you can basically convince anyone to tell you anything. Gossip from your friend, preferred customer sales dates from sales attendants, where they keep the extra free peanuts from the flight attendant…you get the idea. Sweet talk yourself into perks and valuable info.

How to Persuade People

The ability to influence someone during a conversation and make a decision is necessary in order to become one of the most important people in the world today. This ability is useful in business negotiations, and in everyday life.

In general, the impact on people is not so obvious. The basic idea is that people's behavior is often guided by their subconscious simple desires. And to achieve your goals, you need to understand the simple desires of people, and then make your interlocutor passionately wish for something.

It should be noted that in order to influence people you should NOT try to impose or force them to make a hasty decision. It may seem incredible, but the person that wants to reach a mutually beneficial cooperation becomes a huge advantage compared to those that are trying to impose something on others. If you are willing to put yourself in the shoes of another person from whom you want to get something and understand his/her thoughts, then you do not have to worry about your relationship with the person.

The secret lies in the ability to help the self-affirmation of the interlocutor. It is necessary to make sure that your companion looks decent in his own eyes. First things first, there are six basic principles that will absolutely affect any of your interlocutors.

To achieve their goals, people often use the influence of psychology, which helps to manipulate man. Even in ancient times it can be seen that priests ruled the people, instilling in them that religion is harsh, and everyone will be punished if they cannot follow the established rules and practices. Psychological influence strongly acts on the subconscious, causing the victim being influenced to be led by a skilled manipulator.

If you want to succeed and learn how to manage people, these words of the great American entrepreneur should be your credo. You will grow your personality only when you are in close cooperation with the community. From childhood we develop the basic patterns of behavior and outlook, produced by the long historical, biological and mental development of humankind.

In order to have influence and control over another person, it is required that you know their personality and behavioral traits. Most importantly, learn how to use this knowledge to master the specific methods and techniques of influence and control the behavior of the other, on the basis of his outlook, character, personality type and other important psychological features.

If you want to learn how to manage people, secret techniques in this article will let you know not only the theoretical aspect of the question but also allow the use of this knowledge in real life.

To help people to look beyond the limits of consciousness, professionals use a variety of methods and techniques. One of the most effective of these is hypnosis. This method of direct influence on the psyche, whose essence consists of the introduction of human narrowed state of consciousness, makes it is easy to control someone else's suggestion and management.

The ability to manage people, primarily, is to combine the knowledge of human psychology and their personal characteristics. They help to change their own behavior so that this change will cause the desired reaction in others. Try to be more observant while communicating; it will help you better understand the individual psychological characteristics of the interlocutor. Based on this knowledge, try using the following methods and techniques that will help you manage people correctly and efficiently.

To learn how to manipulate people, you must know how it feels to be on both sides. After all, you need to understand the feelings and emotions experienced by each side. This section of the learning process will be much more efficient!

Just focus on the moral side of the issue. If you are ashamed to receive from people that are important to you, you do not accept selfish purposes - better close and do not hurt their highly moral consciousness of the information received.

Chapter 5 Mind Control With NLP To Get What You Want

Mind Control and Brainwashing

Mind control involves manipulation, but the manipulator tries to be friendly to gradually win over the victim while brainwashing is the act of forcibly convincing someone to adopt specific ideas contrary to their beliefs. In brainwashing, coercion and force are typically used. In both cases, Mind control or brainwashing can take place either with or without the victim realizing it, but in most cases, the victims come to the realization of their victimization after mind control, and brainwashing has befallen them.

People can be brainwashed through the following ways: isolation, confrontations on self-esteem, Us vs. Them, Blind Obedience, and Testing.

Isolation

Isolation is the act of separating a person from the world, most notably people close to them so that they solely rely on you as their trusted source of information. Isolation is a means of brainwashing an individual by bringing them more closely to you than their previously trusted close associates. The victimizer attempts to cut off any possible ties with the victim's close associates such, as family members and friends at times, by even discouraging contacts with them and convincing the victim that they are of no use at all. The manipulators are usually aware that the family members would try to warn the victim by implying that they are in a cult or even some dangerous relationships and so they prevent it. They make their victims feel more loved and cared for with them than with their families. In most cases, isolation is accompanied by changes in behavior such as changing names, dressing in a different manner, changing their way of talking, and designing a different hairstyle. This gradually gives the manipulator total domination over the victim in question.

In this case, the manipulator behaves in a friendly manner towards the victim to earn their trust. They usually befriend the victim, making them feel loved and important members of society. Once the manipulator has succeeded in winning their trust, he/she often tries to distance them from their previous close associates. The victim's social activities are controlled in terms of who they interact with, where they go and who they see. The manipulator needs you alone, and at your weakest point when you are away from your close family and friends, they break you. Controlling a victim's mind involves the isolation of the victim. This is a clear indication that the manipulator is trying to win your state of mind.

Confrontations on Self-Esteem

The manipulator conflicts with the intended victim on his/her behavior with the aim of lowering their self-esteem and how they picture themselves. They try to convince the victim that their behaviors are better compared to those of the victims. They often utter terms such as, "this is childish, "this is stupid" or even "not this way" which lower the personality of the victim. The victim, therefore, begins to feel embarrassed about who they are and hence makes an attempt to please the manipulator by doing what they want.

Us vs. Them

The "Us vs. Them" initiative is a way used by manipulators to have their victims chooses between them or others forcibly. The victims only have two choices in this case. Most probably, each choice is accompanied by its consequences. The manipulator makes the situation seem as if the consequences of not choosing them will be disastrous compared to the results of not selecting the other party. The "other party" in this case may refer to any other group but, most probably, the close associates of the victim. The victims, therefore, have no choice but to pledge their loyalty to the manipulator.

Blind Obedience

Blind obedience is the act of following specific set rules to the latter, even if the practices are contrary to one's way of doing things. The manipulator tries to make the victim do as he/she wishes by first making them earn their complete trust. The victim, on the other hand, will do as instructed without even realizing that they are being subjected to mind control. Blind obedience, in many cases, commences the very moment the manipulator gains the complete trust of the victim. The victim, therefore, ends up doing many things, most of which are immoral simply because they were asked to do so. It is most likely that at this point, the victim in question trusts the manipulator so much that he/she doesn't entertain warnings from any concerned individuals. Blind obedience is a total subjection which is more or less the same as a cult. In many cases, manipulators who make victims blindly obey them are usually pathological liars and should never be trusted.

Testing

The manipulator intentionally seeks ideas from the victim, after which he/she deliberately consents to them. This is aimed at raising a sense of victory in the victim. The victim, therefore, feels more secure and comfortable with the manipulator with the impression that the manipulator is the only one that appreciates their efforts. Little do the victims realize that such tests are barely genuine. Such a continuous act by the manipulator leads to the destruction and brainwashing of the victim.

Mind control incidences usually involve teachers or close friends, and the victim believes typically that the manipulator has their best interest at heart. They typically provide private information willingly. The manipulators often control the minds of their victims using different methods. They do this through isolation, moody behavior, metacommunication, Neuro-linguistic programming, and uncompromising rules.

Moody Behavior

Moody behavior is a scenario whereby a manipulator tries to exercise mind control over someone through their actions. As a result of the change in moods, the victim pours out his/her mind to the manipulator without realizing this as a form of brain control. Just because the manipulator can't get his/her ways, he/she showcases a change in behavior contrary to their normal behavior. It is this act that eventually pushes the target victim to change their actions to please the manipulator. Moody behavior as a means of using mind control against an individual is observed among couples, siblings, or even colleagues.

Metacommunication

Metacommunication implies the giving of clues using nonverbal cues in mind control. Whatever an individual says is way contrary to what the sign language he/she is using means. A proper example of this situation is when a parent intends to send her child on an errand. The child will probably say yes in obedience to the parent but then not submissively. He/she may shrug the shoulders, which is certainly a clear indication that there is no willingness in this. Such action will communicate a message to the parent, after which she can decide to withdraw the task. The parent has not withdrawn the task because she wanted to but because her child is not comfortable with it. Therefore, in such a case, the parent is the victim while the child is the manipulator. The intended action is ignored by the victim simply because the manipulator has provided a clue through nonverbal cues.

Neuro-Linguistic Programming

Neuro refers to neurology, linguistic relates to language, and so neuro-linguistic programming refers to how the neuro language works. Commonly termed as NLP. NLP can, therefore, be termed as the instilling of thoughts in the unconscious mind of an individual. This can affect the victim's response. The victim will agree to a situation solely for the sake of it and not because he/she understood the complete details. The manipulator uses this as a means of controlling the mind of the victim. A teacher may introduce a new subject to his students; for example, a French class and being their first day in a French class, the students will take time to grasp the ideas being introduced. At the end of the lesson the teacher may assume that the students understood the lesson yet they actually did not, and most probably he may conclude the lesson by asking "are we together up to this point?" the students will give a "YES" response not because they understood but because at the time the question is asked they are in their unconscious state of mind which is just a goal-getter.

Uncompromising Rules

These are rules and conditions set by a manipulator to control the mind of the victim. These conditions are rules that restrict the behavior of the victim since he/she can only act or speak within limits set. Such rules may include the number of times one has to shower in a day, the language one should speak, the people one should communicate with, the geographical boundaries not to trespass, the time of arrival at home, and even the clothes to be worn among many other restrictions. A person confined to such rules is under obligation to abide by them. His/her behaviors and state of mind is definitely under control. Such a person is not even entitled to making decisions concerning his/her own life. Uncompromising rules subjects one to more than just mind control. The manipulator has now taken the obligation to think and make decisions for you since you can no longer think for yourself and stand on your own choices.

Mind control can be prevented through the following ways: Gain control over any situation, don't do whatever you feel compelled to do, don't let the dynamite explode before you put it out and be an action taker.

Gain Control over Any Situation

Among the ways of preventing mind control is by having control over the situation in your own hands. At times you must handle the situation without any influence from anyone. Divert the locus of power to your direction so that no one thinks for you or makes your decisions. Every human is obliged to individual rights and freedoms, and therefore nobody is entitled to deprive you of them. There is no relationship tie that restricts decision making to just one of the parties involved. Face any situation that comes your way with a lot of boldness and confidence so that nobody takes control of your mind. One should realize that some situations need your own opinion and power, and no one else's. It may not be possible to change the situation at large, let's say the economy or even a particular country's rules and regulations, but what is possible and even much interesting is that you can always choose to change things at your personal level. Take control and step up for your liberty before anyone else partakes your role.

Don't Do Whatever You Feel Compelled to Do

Anytime you feel uncomfortable with handling a situation, do not force yourself into it. Just as Adam Smith once mentioned that a free man works more willingly than a forced man, so be it. Never pressurize yourself into something you are not willing to do. At times the pressure may be accompanied by threats of maybe losing your job, but still, you have to stand on your ground. The decision is yours to make and so let no situation or person control your mind. On many occasions, employees have saved their jobs just because they felt like there was no other choice, rather than getting involved in the dirty job they were asked to do. Be that one employee who would rather lose his/her job but maintain a clear conscience. We are our owners, and so whenever something feels wrong, we have the right to keep the distance. We have the power in our hands to do what we can and not do what we cannot. Whatever wrong that we do when we play victims to our manipulators will always haunt us and thus controlling our minds unless we clear our conscience.

Don't Let the Dynamite Explode Before You Put It Out

At times as human beings, we find ourselves in tough situations and decide to ignore them. Before any situation gets out of hand, it is wise to handle it and be done with it rather than putting it off for another day, which eventually will always remain undecided. Just as dynamite explodes, so will the situation in question, and for the effects, they will be destructive. There is no need to stay silent over what has already taken place. Just be bold enough to spell it out, no matter the consequences. Once we ignore a pressing issue, there have to be some things that we can't do because we are compelled by the problem we do not want to talk about. This takes control of our mind, and in some cases, other parties use it as a tool for blackmail. It is better to face the situation before it gets too late. Sometimes we do not express ourselves because of the fear imposed on us, but it's just okay. Speak out no matter the threats. If you are faced with a situation where you happen to witness a murder incident by chance, and then you decide to stay silent about it. Unfortunately, sometime later, the CCTV footage reveals your presence in the scene, and you get arrested not necessarily because you were the murderer but because you are considered an accomplice to the murder by not having opened up to the authorities on time.

Be an Action Taker

As an individual, you need to be aggressive despite the changes that take place in your life. Take action rather than just sitting back and waiting for nothing in particular. Whenever one door in your life is shut, make an effort to open another one. The closure of one entry does not necessarily imply failure or giving up. Let the closed door not be an obstacle set to control your thinking and behavior. Stand up and own yourself. Maintain the everyday energy and assure yourself that you can handle the situation. For instance, when you lose your job, take action. Wake up early daily and carry out your daily routines as you try to figure out new ventures. Whenever you fall into any trap, that is just a bare reminder that you need to be extra careful. Be an action taker, and make sure to watch your steps keenly before any action. The situation is always in your hands. If you don't take action, then no one will.

The effects of brainwashing and mind control have mostly affected a considerable percentage of the world's population in recent years. In most cases, the victims are usually not aware of the incidences of brainwashing, and if so, are usually in denial of the fact that they are being used as objects of manipulation. It is wiser to open up to any trusted associate when you become a victim of brainwashing, for it may cause psychological issues if not handled appropriately. It is important to stay alert and be safe away from manipulators because, in most cases, the manipulators come in different unknown ways. Stick to your family members and only to your trusted friends. Better still, free yourself from any situations that might make you vulnerable and seem to be getting out of hand. Kindly stay alert.

Chapter 6 Protecting Oneself from NLP Mind Control

Principles of NLP

From neurolinguistic programming, we will take the principles and strategies useful for our purposes.

Eye movements

Let's start with the known eye movements. Our brain is divided into two hemispheres with different and complementary competences. The left hemisphere, logical / digital, is the site of the areas responsible for language. The right is analog / emotional and controls the ability to orient ourselves in space. The left hemisphere controls the right part of the body, while the right hemisphere controls the left part. The eye movements at the top indicate a visual representation (mental image). The level movements (neither above nor below), to the right or to the left, are an indication of an auditory construct. Movements (both up and down) to the right indicate constructed (visual or auditory) representations. The ocular shifts to the left (up or level) indicate images or sounds (sounds, noises, words), remembered. Example: if a person is absorbed in the memory of an episode, his eyes will be oriented to his left (up and / or level). Rarely, the eyes, even if the person actually remembers the episodes, remain fixed forward.

Example: if a person imagines having sex with Sophia Loren, his eyes will turn to his right (up and / or level). By level, I mean moving horizontally to the right or to the left.

Lower eye movements:

To the left = internal dialogue

To the right = bodily sensations, cenesthetic access

Internal dialogue is the type of conversation we do mentally.

Tracing and guide

Tracing means tracking (copying, imitating, etc.) a posture, a movement or a complete mental strategy. You can trace everything, breathing, posture, tone of voice, etc. The trace itself creates empathy and agreement. Once I have traced, it is possible to lead.

Example: 1) I trace my partner's breath

2) as I got in synchronicity, I try to change my breathing and see if the person follows me instinctively. If he follows, you are already leading.

Anchors

Anchors are used to fix a behavior, an emotional state or a decision-making strategy. To anchor, we must first decide what we want. Do we want to seduce a girl? In the interaction, look for a mood, emotion or behavior that seems useful to seduce her.

Example: A girl tells you about an old love, getting showily excited . If you find it useful to anchor this emotional state (it depends on the purpose and use you want to make of it. Perhaps there is too much anger and pain in the emotional state that relives), it will be enough to associate it with a "stimulus."

To anchor you can use one or more nonverbal channels. There are four basic nonverbal channels: kinesics, proxemics, digital and paralinguistics. The advice for anchors is to use digital or paralinguistics media (or both). Paralinguistics: vocal sounds (also the tone of voice).

Digital: touch

Example: While a woman is in the state you want to anchor, touch her at a point on the body and, at the same time, use a lower tone of voice. To anchor well, both touch and tone must be "characteristic" (do not use socially available areas - hands, hips, thighs). Anchor with finger pressure (like claws) on the neck, shoulders or forehead. The head of women is the least touched area by men. If you still do not have the confidence to anchor in these areas, you will use your arms or only your tone of voice (even a coughing, a snort or other sounds are useful for anchoring).

Once you have anchored, test the anchor. When you find it useful, drop the anchor. Simply repeat the stimulus you have previously associated. Remember to touch the person in the same place, with the same pressure and same fingers' position.

Precision will help a lot. The same applies to tone of voice or vocal sounds. If the anchor has been perfectly made, you just have to repeat the stimulus (drop the anchor) to generate the repetition of the emotional state / decision. Actually, you have established a "conditioned reflex ".

Interrupting the pattern

Interrupting patterns is a technique used in hypnotic inductions. Interrupting an instinctive pattern, such as handshaking or lighting a cigarette, causes a judgment and behavior suspension that allows the addition of an order (suggestion). Time for this suspension is short.

In our daily relationships, this procedure is unrealizable. Only in a seductive and sexual environment is it possible to use it, thanks to the particular confidence and the type of "game" that lovers use to play. Lovers play, chase each other, pretend to be offended, want to choke their beloved. In such a relational framework, the interruption of the scheme is a piece of cake.

Eye movements and anchors

At the beginning we talked about eye movements, which give us information about the type of access (visual, auditory, kinesthetic, etc.). In addition to being useful in the extraction phase (where information are collected), the eye movements can be anchored and used at the right time. For our purposes it is useless to examine this issue in depth. Since the eye movements tell us what a person thinks, we can use them in our favor.

Example: We ask a girl out. We notice that before answering, move your eyes up to the right and then down to the right. What can we deduce from this? That she first built an image (she was with us in the restaurant, in the car, etc.) followed by a feeling / emotion.

If this feeling is positive, we will have the opportunity to meet her. Mental strategies can be very complex (with many eye movements before the decision), but the key is the last access you experience before deciding. If a person has a kinesthetic as the last access to a decision-making strategy and you have already anchored one before, use it (pull the anchor).

Remember and guide eye movements

Example: A customer is deciding whether to buy a new living room. The eyes move up to the right and then down to the left. In this case, he first built an image and then had an internal dialogue (a talk with yourself). If the person is undecided, we can trace the strategy and guide him to the purchase.

Example of layout and orientation: imagine how you will stay at home (induction of the built image). I have the same model at home (empathy). Every time I sit there I think: "such a good purchase" (track and guide the internal dialogue). Example: the customer looks first up to the left and then down to the right, going from a chest breath to a low (abdominal). A high or chest breathing is typical of a visual person or a visual access. Abdominal breathing indicates kinesthetic access in addition to being a characteristic of kinesthetic individuals. In the last example, the client first accesses a remembered image and then has a kinesthetic access (decision key). This time, when drawing the strategy, we will use our fingers to guide the look and facilitate tracking. Example: moving the arm up to your right, say: these objects are no longer found, they remind me... (tracing verbal and kinetic). Move the right arm down to the left: what a pleasant feeling, it is a very beautiful vintage piece of furniture. It can be tracked and guided, either verbally or nonverbally.

In relationships, where you have more time, we can create more anchors and then use them at the right time.

Verse and away from

There are individuals who move towards situations, people and things, others that move away from them.

The first seek pleasure, well-being, success, satisfaction, recognition. The latter avoid pain, tension, shame, boredom, danger.

This metaprogram in the NLP is the verse or away from. The verse moves towards the things that they consider positive.

The away from avoid the things that they consider negative.

It is a matter of focus. Even in the language we realize

Verse: I want, I have chosen, I like it, I can't wait, etc.

Away from: I don't want to, I don't like it, I would like to avoid it, I'm afraid etc.

The versos focus on reaching and conquering their goals. They are impulsive and act without thinking too much about it.

Motivate them: underline the advantages and the feeling of success in making an action or decision. The measures they take are focus on the possible negative consequences or difficulties they may encounter to meet their own needs. They are very thoughtful and take time to act. To motivate them: point out the disadvantages and dangers of not making a decision or acting.

Many times, whether you are conscious of it or not, people will try to use NLP mind control on you to have you become submissive to them. This will include those you work with and those you get into intimate relationships with. Though, developing a keen and potent immunity to it will be of much help to you.

To do this, you must closely study the mechanics that are employed by experts in the field. Here are ways of protecting oneself from NLP mind control:

Be very wary of those who copy your body language:

When you are talking to a person that you suspect may be into NLP and you note that they are trying to copy some of your gestures and mannerisms by either trying to sit the way you sit or trying to place their hands the way you have placed yours, put them to test by making a few adjustments to the way you sit by changing the way you have placed some parts of your body to see if they will do the same.

For those who are skilled in the art of NLP, they will find it much easier to mask this than those who are new to it, as the new ones tend to copy the movement of the body almost immediately after you do so. When you notice such mirroring of your gestures, it is time to raise a point of order to let them know that they are beginning to cross the line.

Make random unpredictable patterned movements with your eyes:

You will find that this is a very funny way to troll NLPers, but for what it's worth you should try it out, especially when your rapport with the NLP user is at its initial stage. At this stage, they will generally try their best to pay keen attention to your eyes. You may be deceived into thinking that their attention to your eyes is because they have an interest in what you have to say.

Maybe they are interested in what you are saying but this is not because they are interested in your thought process. The attention they give to your eye movement is because they want to study and know the way you store and process certain information.

Watching the movement of your eyes will give them certain information about you, such that in a few minutes, they will be able to easily decode when you are not telling the truth and even the part of the brain you use whenever you are speaking. This will give them so much insight into what your thoughts are, such that they will even appear to have some psychic information about your core thoughts.

To break this, you can begin to dart your eyes around whenever you speak with people that you suspect of using NLP so that you frequently look up, down and sideways. You can make it look as if this is a natural thing for you to do when you talk to people but at the same time, try to do it randomly without a pattern. This will make the NLP user go crazy as you will be doing so much to throw their calibration off balance.

Avoid being touched by anyone:

This may be an obvious practice, but it should be done with more caution when you are having a conversation with a person whom you suspect may be into NLP. This is an especially important practice whenever you find yourself in a heightened emotional state of anger or laughter or anything like that and the person you are having a conversation with attempts to touch you at a point when you are still in that state.

For example, they may choose to tap you on the shoulder. If they do this, they would have successfully anchored you so that if they desire to make you go back to that state later, they can just touch you on the same spot. This is as suggested by NLP's wayward logic.

Beware of vague language:

One of NLP's core techniques, which it adopts from Milton Erickson, is its use of vague language to initiate a hypnotic trance. Erickson discovered that the vaguer the language, the easier it is to lead people into a trance. This is a result of the fact that the person has less information to disagree with or even react to.

On the other hand, more specific language would easily take a person out of a trance. Take note of the language of politicians. For instance, Obama's "change" mantra is a good example of this technique, as the word is so vague that different people can easily read different meanings to it.

Pay attention to permissive language:

Be wary of those that are prone to use such permissive phrases like "feel free to relax," "you are welcome to look at my new apartment if you like," "you can have it for as long as you like," etc. This is an early indication of a pre-NLP hypnotist like Erickson himself.

The best way to have someone do a thing or two, or go into a trance, is by making them give you permission to do so. This is true because a skilled hypnotist will never go the route of commanding you straight-up to do their will. You will never hear them say things like "go into a trance," but you will often hear them say things like "you are free to relax as much as you want."

Beware of gibberish:

Pay keen attention to people who make phrases that may not really make sense when you pay close attention to their words. Gibberish is the core factor of both the pacing and the leading phase of the NLP. The hypnotist is not actually saying anything, what they do is to shape your emotional state in such a way that it moves you to the place that they want you to go.

To counter this, you can always ask them to be more specific about what they are saying or to explain what they mean by what they have said. What this does is to throw their technique off balance and ensures that the conversation goes in a specific order, with a specific language by breaking the trance. This includes the use of vague language.

Always read between the lines:

Those who use NLP will always use words or phrases with some hidden or covert meanings. On the surface their language, when heard quickly, will come across as though it is an obvious statement that you do not have to think deeply about before agreeing with.

For example, if a person says "diet, nutrition and sleep with me are very important things, don't you think?" you may, on the surface, agree with the fact that diet, nutrition, and sleep are indeed important, and it is a good thing that the person is paying attention to their health. So, without paying attention, you have already agreed with them but what about the layered message which lies in the phrase "diet and sleep with me." Without knowing it, you have already agreed to it. This is a very subtle art that is common with skilled NLP users.

Maintain your attention:

You need to be careful when you are around NLP users to ensure that you do not zone out around them. This means that you must go into every interaction with them with a conscious cue.

For example, if an NLP user is trying to get you to work for them for free, the moment they notice that you are not really paying attention to them, and have begun to zone out, they will begin to use the technique to tell you about how lucky they are to never have to pay for any service because they always get people to do it for free. They will ensure that they ring this keyword into your head in order to change your mindset without you knowing it.

Try to not agree to anything:

If you find out that you have been put under pressure to make quick decisions and it begins to feel like you are being steered in a certain direction, try your best to leave the situation. Give yourself time, wait as long as 24 hours or more if necessary before you make any decisions, especially ones that have to do with your finances.

Be careful to not be swept up to the point where you must make decisions based on your emotions in the spur of the moment. This is a common tool in the hands of salespeople who are always armed with different NLP techniques with the aim of making you buy on impulse. Always have it at the back of your mind that you do not have to do what they want you to do. Take a walk, breathe and make use of your rational mind.

Always trust your intuition:

This is the basic, most important rule. Whenever you feel like a person may be messing with you or when you feel uneasy with a person, trust your gut feelings. NLP users will always seem off and dodgy. Stay as far away from such people as you can or be clear about the fact that you demand that they respect you enough to not apply NLP techniques whenever they are communicating with you.

As annoying and pernicious as NLP can be, it is possible to resist this modern day "black magic." You will always come across NLP users in different areas of your daily interactions. You may not be able to avoid them if you listen to politicians, interact with marketers or even when you walk into a used car sales lot. Arming yourself with this list will help you to avoid their gimmicks. You will be surprised at how much more aware you become of their techniques.

Chapter 7 What Is Dark Psychology And How To Use It To Influence People

Dark psychology is the art of using manipulation and mind control over others. It is the study of human conditions about how people prey on others. We all have the potential to oppress other human beings and creatures. Most of us restrain this feeling, but some utilize it. Dark psychology tries to find out the perceptions, behaviors, and thoughts that lead to this preying behavior. In most cases, dark psychology has found that 99.99% is goal-oriented, and the remaining 0.01% manipulate others with no purpose and with no influence from religious dogma and science. Therefore, dark psychology is the trend in which people use techniques like persuasion, manipulation, and motivation to get their way. What is a dark psychology triad?

Dark psychology triad is the seeking to foretell the criminal behavior and manipulation in relationships. These triads are narcissism, which is the grandiosity, egotism, and lacking empathy, psychopathy, which is using charm and friendliness, but lacking empathy, selfishness, and remorsefulness to get what you want and Machiavellianism, which is manipulating others with deception and lacking morality in your manipulation. Nobody wants to be manipulated, but in today's world, we are prone to be manipulated. It does not have to be in extreme cases like the dark triad above, but we are manipulated in simple actions that may seem harmless and normal. You will find this manipulation in sales techniques, in the internet ads, and our children when they seek to get what they want. People we love and trust a lot apply dark psychology to us.

Dark psychology involves everything that human beings are in their dark part. We all have a masked side within us from birth that is evil. Dark psychology has found out that these people who do these acts never do it for sex, power, retribution, or any other purpose. They commit these heinous acts with no goal in mind. They violate and harm others just for the thrill of it. We all have that potential in us. The potential to harm others without explanation or reason. Dark psychology takes this potential to be difficult and complex to explain. Let us look at the 0.01% manipulators in dark psychology.

Predator - This is a person or persons who exploit, victimize, stalk, or coerce others using information in technology. They have desires and fantasies to control and get power. Predators can be of any age and gender who indulge in cyberstalker, cyberbully, internet troll, cyber-terrorist, online psychopath, or who engages in internet defamations.

Arsonist - This is a person who is obsessed with fire and its settings. These types of people have a history of physical and sexual abuse. Most arsonists are loners, have few peers, and are impressed by fire. They are ritualistic and set fires on a pattern. They get their targets and set it ablaze to get sexual arousal and feel proud.

Necrophilia - These are people with disorders and have a sexual attraction to dead people. They have a problem and get sexually attracted to things or corpses.

Chapter 8 How To Hypnotize A Person

Hypnosis

Although brainwashing is a very common mind control method that so many people may already be aware of, there is also an important type of mind control that many people may be aware of. This is known as hypnosis and should be given as much importance as the others.

Generally, most of those that know a thing or two about hypnosis get their knowledge from stage plays where the actors perform ridiculous acts. What is seen in plays is also a type of hypnosis, but there is a lot more to it than what is portrayed in these shows.

Hypnosis, according to experts, comes from a state of consciousness dealing with focused attention and the reduction of awareness on the peripheral level, which deals with the ability of the participant to give a response to the suggestions that are given. What this entails is the participant transcending to an entirely different state of mind, making them more susceptible to taking and acting on all the suggestions that the hypnotist makes.

There are two different theories that attempt to explain what really goes on during the period of hypnosis. The first is known as the altered-state theory. Those that belong to this school of thought are of the opinion that hypnosis is like a trance or a state of the mind where the target discovers that their state of awareness is different from what they would ordinarily notice when they are conscious. The second theory is the non-state theory, which is of the opinion that people who are hypnotized do not necessarily have to go into another state of consciousness. Those that belong to this school of thought believe that the hypnotist works with the target to enact an imaginative role.

When a person is hypnotized, he learns to gain more concentration and focus that is combined with a newly learned ability to concentrate a great deal to a certain memory or thought. When they are in this state, the participant will be able to filter through and block any source of distraction. Those that are hypnotized are thought to be able to exhibit a high ability to respond to all the suggestions they receive, especially when the hypnotist is the source of that suggestion.

The process used to get the target to enter the state of hypnosis is known as hypnotic induction and usually has to do with several suggestions and instructions that serve as a tool for warming up.

Different experts hold different opinions concerning what the definition of hypnosis is. This wide range of definitions comes from the fact that there is an avalanche of circumstances that following the state of hypnosis. Two different people cannot possibly have the same experience when they are being hypnotized.

Below are some of these different definitions of hypnosis:

• Michael Nash says it is a special case of psychological regression.

• Ernest and Janet Hilgard, who have written extensively on the topic of hypnosis, say it is a way that the body detaches from itself into a different plane of consciousness.

• Two well-known social psychologists, Sarbin and Coe, use role theory as a term to describe hypnosis. In this definition, the participant is the one that plays the role of being hypnotized. They believe that the participants are not actually in a state of being hypnotized, rather, they are acting as though they are hypnotized.

• Hypnosis is defined by T.X. Barber in non-hypnotic behavioral parameters. In this definition, the participant is said to give a definition to the task motivation and then tag the situation they find themselves in as hypnosis since they do not have any other name for the state they are in.

• In some of Weitzenhoffer's earlier writings on hypnosis, he described hypnosis as a state where a person's suggestibility is enhanced. In some of his more recent writings, he goes further to define hypnosis as an act where one person influences the other by exerting his influence on the other person with a suggestion as a medium or agency.

- In Brennan and Gill's definition, a psychoanalytic concept which is known as "regression in an ego's service" is used in describing the whole essence of hypnosis. In this definition, the target is very ready to submit himself to a state of hypnosis because it helps to boost their ego and makes them feel better.

- Edmonston is of the belief that when a person enters a state of hypnosis, they are simply destressing in a state of relaxation.

- Spiegel and Spiegel also add their voice to the topic, stating that hypnosis has nothing to do with the biological capacity of the participant, as it is just something that happens.

- Erickson thinks that hypnosis is an altered, inner-directed and a special state where people function. According to him, the participant in a state of hypnosis will still can function and take note of things that are happening around them, but this is not as it is in their normal state since it is an altered state.

When it comes to hypnosis, different people hold different opinions and views about the topic. There are those who think that hypnosis is a real phenomenon and they are often paranoid about the possibility of the government or other bodies trying to take control of their minds. Other people think that there is no such thing as hypnosis, so they think that it is merely slight of the hand. It is quite possible that hypnosis is a mind control tool that falls between the two schools of thought.

In the psychological community, three stages of hypnosis are identified. These three stages are induction, suggestion and susceptibility. Each one of these stages is as important to the process of hypnosis as the other.

Induction:

This is the first stage of hypnosis. It is the phase that happens before the participant fully goes into hypnosis. They are always introduced to a technique known as the hypnotic induction technique. Over many years, psychologists thought this was a tactic used in making the subject to go into a hypnotic trance. This definition has changed the view of some psychologists in modern times. According to some of the non-state theorists, this state can be viewed from a slightly different angle. According to them, this stage is one that heightens the expectations of the participants concerning the things that are going to happen. Here they try to give a definition to the role that they are going to play and try to get themselves to focus their attention in the right direction. This stage also puts the participant through any other step that will help him go in the right direction for hypnosis.

There are many different induction techniques that are used during hypnosis but the most recognized and influential is Braid's 'eye fixation' technique, otherwise known as Braidism. This approach has many different applications, including the Stanford Hypnotic Susceptibility Scale (SHSS), which is the most common tool when it comes to hypnosis.

To make use of SHSS, you are required to follow a couple of steps. The first of these steps is to find an object that is bright, like a watch, then place it between your middle finger and your thumb finger in your left hand. It is best for you to hold this object about eight to fifteen inches away from the eyes of the person that is to be hypnotized. It should be placed anywhere above the person's forehead so that it can produce a lot of strain to their eyelids and eyes during the process, and such that the participant will always be able to fix their gaze on the object. Make sure you tell the participants that they must stare at the object.

They also need to create an idea for that object then focus their mind completely on that idea. They should not think of any other thing at this point or let their mind's eye drift to the thought of whether the process is going to be successful. If this is done properly, the eyes of the participants will begin to dilate after a short time, and within a little more time they will begin to move in a wavy motion.

At the point when the middle and the forefingers of the left hand are moved away from the object, the participant is likely to close their eyes involuntarily. If this happens, it means that the participant has entered a trance. If they don't, then the process will have to be repeated for the participant and they should be made aware that they are expected to close their eyes as soon as the fingers are moved in the same motion. This will then allow them to enter the hypnotic state.

Although Braid stood firmly by this technique, he agreed that the use of the induction technique of hypnosis may not be required for every case. As a matter of fact, it was discovered recently that the induction technique does not have any effect on the hypnotic suggestion as experts were earlier made to believe (Smith 2014). Over many years, there were some other variations and alternatives of the initial version of the hypnotic induction technique even though Braid's technique was regarded as the best.

Suggestion:

This is the second phase of hypnosis which is known as the suggestion stage. It is worthy of note that at the point when Braid first talked about hypnosis, he didn't make any mention of the term "suggestion." Rather, he referred to this second phase as the stage where the participant focuses their conscious mind on a dominant idea.

Braid was able to do this by stimulating or reducing the function of the person's psychological functioning in different parts of the body of the participant. He later began to place even more emphasis on the possibility some verbal and non-verbal forms of suggestion to be able to get the participant's mind into a hypnotic state. This hypnotic state of the mind will include making use of "waking suggestions" and self-hypnosis.

Hippolyte Bernheim, another popular hypnotist, also proceeded in making a shift on the emphasis of the physical state of the hypnosis process to the psychological process that has to do with verbal suggestions. According to him, the art of hypnotism is the induction of a certain physical condition that is spectacular and that will boost the susceptibility of any suggestion the hypnotist makes to the participant. Many times, the hypnotic state that is already induced is going to help in facilitating the suggestion the hypnotist makes. In modern hypnotism, a lot of different forms of suggestions are used to achieve success such as insinuations, metaphors, non-verbal or indirect suggestions, direct verbal suggestions and other similar figures of speech and suggestions that do not come in a verbal form. Some of these paralinguistic suggestions may be used during the suggestion stage and all have to do with manipulation, mental imagery and the voice tonality. One of the differences in the types of suggestion that the participant will be offered includes the suggestions that are given with permission or the ones that are given in a more authoritarian manner.

One of the major things that should be considered when it comes to the topic of hypnosis is the point of diversion between the conscious and the unconscious mind. For many hypnotists, the suggestion stage is viewed as a means of communication that is directed mostly towards the subject's conscious mind. There are some others who hold an opposing view to this though. According to these other hypnotists, there is a communication between the agent and the subconscious or unconscious mind. However, Bernheim, Braid and other hypnotists that existed in the Victorian age believed that any suggestion at all is delivered straight up to the consciousness of the participant's mind rather than the unconscious part of the mind. Braid further defines the act of hypnotism as the focused attention on either the suggestion or the idea that is more dominant.

Most people fear that the hypnotists will have access to their subconscious state and will be able to influence them to do and think things that they will not be able to control. This fear is quite baseless as according to those that go with the train thought, it is simply not possible. When it comes to the different conceptions about the suggestion, the nature of the mind is also a determining factor. There are some people who hold the belief that the responses given are from the unconscious mind, such was the case of Milton Erickson. This brings up other cases of the use of indirect suggestions, like in stories or metaphors. Many of these indirect suggestions usually hide their intended meanings so that they can hide from the subject's conscious mind.

There is also a form of hypnosis known as a subliminal suggestion, which relies totally on the theory of the unconscious mind. If it is possible for the unconscious mind to be left out of hypnosis, it wouldn't be possible to have this kind of suggestion. However, it is quite easy to point out the differences between these two. For those that believe that the conscious mind is the primary recipient of the suggestion, stories and metaphors that have hidden meanings will be used. In any of the theories of thought, the subject will have to be able to place his focus on one idea or an object. This will help them to be moved in the direction that they need to go so that they will be able to enter a hypnotic state.

As soon as the suggested state has been successfully entered, the participant will now be able to proceed to the third stage which is the susceptibility stage.

Susceptibility:

Over the years, it was noted that different people have different reactions to hypnosis. There are people who find it easy to fall into the hypnotic trance and do not have to try very hard to fall into it. For other people, even though it may take a prolonged period, they will be able to get into hypnosis if they put in some effort. There are also other people that will not be able to get into the hypnotic trance, even with continued efforts.

The interesting thing that researchers have discovered about the susceptibility of different subjects is that it remains a constant factor. A person that gets into the hypnotic trance easily will likely remain that way for the rest of their life. Similarly, A person that gets into the hypnotic trance with difficulty or one that has never reached the hypnotic state at all will most likely never be hypnotized. Over time, different models have been developed to determine the participant's susceptibility to hypnosis. Some older depth scales have worked to make inferences on the level of the participant's trance using the available signs that were observed. These signs include such things as amnesia. There are some more modern scales that will work for measuring the degree of the self-evaluated or the responsiveness that will be observed to the suggestion tests which are given like the direct suggestions of the rigidity of the arm.

In her research, Deirdre Barrett came up with the idea that two types of subjects exist that are highly susceptible to the effects of hypnosis. These two groups are known as the dissociaters and the fantasizers.

The fantasizers will score very high on the absorption scale and they will be able to block out every stimulus of the outside world easily without making use of hypnosis. This type of person typically spends a good amount of time daydreaming. They will have had imaginary friends in their childhood and are also very likely to have grown up in an environment where there was a lot of encouragement for imaginary play.

On the other hand, those who are dissociated will often emerge from a traumatic background or may have experienced abuse in their childhood. However, they find it easy to get over those unpleasant events and can transition into a state of numbness. Instead of creating fantasies, people in this group would rather go blank when they daydream.

These two groups will score very high when they undergo the test of hypnotic susceptibility and the test will include the difficulties that arises from Post-traumatic Stress Disorder as well as Dissociative Identity Disorder.

Applications of Hypnosis

The concept or field of hypnosis has been in practice for a very long time and as a result of there have been different emerging ways of application which assist in making sure that the process of hypnosis is put to good use.

The application of hypnosis cuts across many fields of life, from entertainment to military uses to self-improvement and even medicine. There are some areas that have only recently begun the use of hypnosis like physiotherapy, forensics, sports and education.

Even artists have begun to use hypnotism to reach some of their creative goals. One of the most well-known examples of such artists is Andre Breton. Breton makes use of hypnosis as well as other techniques to enable him to reach his creative purposes in surrealism.

Hypnosis is also now used widely when it comes to self-improvement as so many people have decided to employ self-hypnosis in order to reach their weight loss goals, to reduce stress or quit smoking. Below are some of the fields where hypnosis have proven to be effective and an explanation of the way the process has been put to work in those fields.

Applications in the Military

Apart from helping individuals battling with various health issues and addictions, various efforts have been made to apply hypnosis to the military field as well. The American military have made an attempt in this regard. According to a top secret but later declassified document that was retrieved through the Freedom of Information Act stores recently, it was proved clearly that the act of hypnosis had already been researched in the military. Sadly, the report from the research showed that there really wasn't any proof that the process of hypnosis would be applicable to the military field. Also, there was no evidence that showed vividly that hypnosis really exists as a real phenomenon aside the subject of high motivation, expectancy, and mere suggestion.

The document explains how it would be difficult if not almost impossible for hypnosis to be applied in the military world. It states:

"The application of hypnosis in intelligence would lead to certain technical challenges that are not encountered in the hospital or medical laboratory. For instance, if you want to obtain compliance from a resistant subject, it would be imperative to hypnotize the subject under certain important hostile conditions. However, there are no good clinical nor experimental evidence that proves that this is possible."

The report from the classified document further explained the difficulty faced when the researchers attempted to study the outcome and possible application of hypnotism in the military. This is because no-one has been able to state with utmost certainty if hypnosis is a unique state with some specific responses or simply a type of suggestion that is produced because of the positive association between the hypnotist and subject.

<u>Hypnosis as a form of therapy (Hypnotherapy)</u>

Hypnotherapy is a form of psychotherapy using the process of hypnosis. This form of therapy is used to help subjects battling with various issues bothering their minds, especially in cases where other forms of therapy such as self-control have proved abortive. Certified psychologists and doctors may try out a form of hypnotherapy on voluntary subjects in a bid to assist the subjects deal with anxiety, post-traumatic stress, insomnia, bulimia, compulsive gambling, and depression.

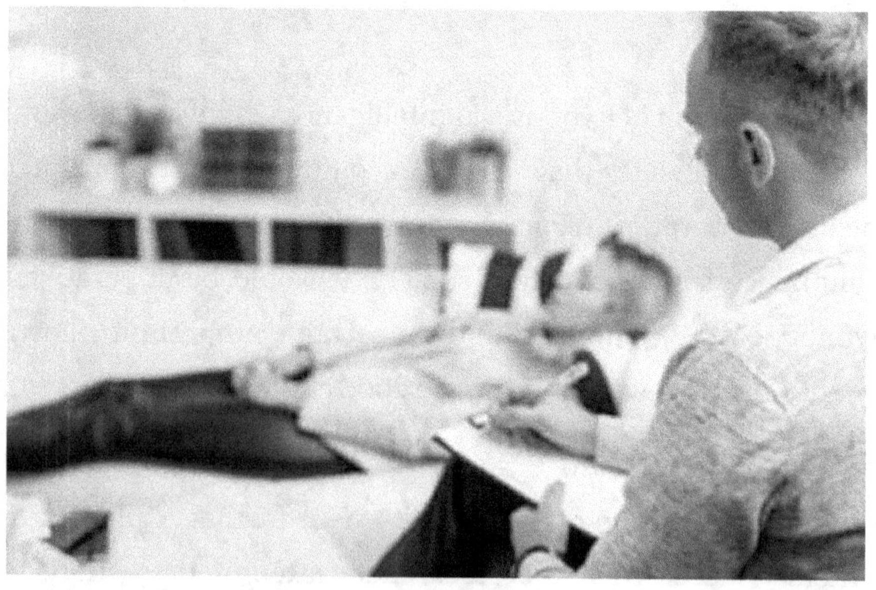

An individual can decide to book a session with a certified hypnotherapist to assist in managing an issue such as help in quitting smoking. It is important to keep in mind that a certified hypnotherapist is neither a psychologist nor a doctor, so they will simply be able to help you get hypnotized but not with a cure to serious illnesses. Therefore, be sure that your hypnotherapist is certified to provide you with these services. Whether to choose a hypnotherapist or a physician is totally up to you.

In modern history, there are various forms of hypnotherapy. Each with a different level of success and depends on the challenges faced by the subject(s). These various forms include:

Cognitive-behavioral hypnotherapy - This is a combination of various elements, cognitive-behavioral therapy and clinical hypnosis;

Hypnoanalysis – Hypnoanalysis is a modern form of regression hypnotherapy;

- Ericksonian hypnotherapy;

- Hypnotherapy to assist with addictions;

- Hypnotherapy can help with soothing patients who are anxious before undergoing surgery;

- Reduce feelings of nausea in cancer patients while treating them with chemotherapy;

- Managing pain during dental care;

- Treating skin diseases such as psoriasis and warts;

- Reducing symptoms of Irritable Bowel Syndrome;

- Hypnotherapy to help athletes improve their performance in a competition;

- Hypnotherapy to help with weight loss;

- Managing chronic pain such as rheumatoid arthritis;

- Managing and alleviating pain associated with childbirth;

- Hypnotherapy can help in dealing with skin diseases;

- Hypnosis to help with management of fears (phobias);

- Hypnotherapy to help with behavioral control;

- Hypnotherapy to help with pain management, especially those suffering from chronic pain;

- Hypnotherapy to can also help with psychological therapy which the patient is battling with;

- Hypnotherapy to aid with relaxation.;

- Minimizing the symptoms observed in those having dementia.

The above are just a few areas where hypnosis can be applied. Although, most people believe that hypnosis can be used as a tool to manipulate a subject and induce them to do horrible things acts or renounce their own faith, all these are mere misconceptions. The most common application of hypnosis is directed towards improving the health of the subject (therapy).

Self-hypnosis

There are some situations in which a qualified hypnotherapist or another expert are not available, and an individual may choose to hypnotize himself. This process can be carried out by using auto-suggestion strategy. The main application of this method is for self-development and most individuals will attempt it in a bid to minimize their stress levels, stop smoking, or to improve their diet. Some individuals find it easy to self-hypnotize, most individuals need some help with getting hypnotized. Such help could include mind machine devices or hypnotic recordings to help them get hypnotized. Other aspects where self-hypnosis is applicable include help in relaxing, to get overcome fear of crowd and with physical well-being.

Stage Hypnosis

Whenever people hear of hypnosis, what comes to mind is stage hypnosis which is a form of entertainment that usually takes place in a club or a theatre in front of a crowd. The performer (hypnotist) is considered as a spectacular showman and this enhances the concept that hypnosis is entirely about manipulation of the mind. At the start of the show, the performer will try to put the entire crowd under an altered state before choosing an individual who fits the criteria to come on the podium and to be subjected to various embarrassing performances under the watch of the crowd.

The reason why stage hypnosis is so effective is still a mystery, though it is widely believed that there is a combination of physical manipulation, stagecraft, trickery, suggestibility, participant selection, and psychological factors. Mainly, experts think that the volunteer is simply conforming to the biddings of the hypnotist and providing a form of entertainment. These volunteers may want to do this because they wish to draw attention to themselves, the desire to satisfy others, and the fear of making it easy to get the volunteer to perform. Some books that were written by some stage hypnotists supports the concept of deception, trickery and some are absolutely made up of false hypnosis where secret whispers were used all through the performance.

Chapter 9 Other Benefits of Hypnosis

Boosting Performance

In our day-to-day life, we are always looking for ways to improve our performance. Many things could hold us back from living our best life and achieving our greatest potential. If we are not careful, we can be held back by the many distractions in our life. One of the ways to increase performance is by indulging in hypnosis. It helps improve our focus and attention and prepares us for success. People who practice hypnosis have reported improved concentration and capacity to utilize their full potential. If one is struggling in any area of your life, be it academics or professional, hypnosis can be helpful.

Healing Anxiety

Let us face it; we live in a world that is full of stimulations everywhere you turn. These stimulations can have a negative impact on the emotional health of an individual. More precisely, they can cause an individual to feel anxious. When you are anxious, most of the time, you are going to be less productive, and have a hard time interacting with other people. However, we are social animals and we need to stay in contact with other people in order to fulfill our important emotional and physical needs. One of the ways to get rid of anxiety is through indulging in hypnosis. This exercise prepares one mentally to overcome the negative emotions and ascend from the bondage of anxiety. It also helps the individual acquire a high level of self-awareness, so that they are aware of who they truly are.

Boosting Self-Confidence

One of the major problems that most people face in the world is a lack of self-confidence. In addition, when one is lacking in self-confidence, it does not matter what their potential might be, but they are not in a position to accomplish their life goals. Before you can succeed, you need the input of other human beings. Then you have to be confident in your capabilities so that other people may come in. So many people end up wasting their potential because of their low self-confidence. One of the best ways to turn around this condition is through practicing hypnosis. In this way, the individual gets a boost in their self-confidence, and finally, they have the power to become who they want to be.

Eradicating Negative Habits

One of the things that stop us from becoming the best version of ourselves is our negative habits. We acquire these negative habits from either spending time with the wrong crowd or consuming negative material. Either way, negative habits affect our productivity and discourage us from being the best we can be. But then overcoming these negative habits is not something you can do at the snap of a finger. One of the exercises you can take to overcome these negative habits is hypnosis. Hypnosis helps kill the urge to revert into your old negative habits.

Helping Stop Addictions

It's one thing to have a negative habit, but it's another thing to have an addiction. When you are addicted to something, it means that you cannot function in a normal way unless you get your fix. Addictions not only kill any potential we might have but they also drive people into early graves. It is very crucial that someone overcomes their addiction because if left untreated soon they are reduced to nothing. Overcoming an addiction through willpower is a tall order. Hypnosis is one exercise that can help you fight away addictions so that you have a new chance to pursue your dreams and be the best you can be. Some terrible addictions that entrap most people include: sex, alcohol, gambling, and video games.

Fighting Away Phobias

If you have a phobia about something, there's a reason behind it. But then phobias stop you from experiencing what life has to offer. Phobias cause you to be affected by things that do not affect normal people. Struggling with phobias means that there are many potential situations you are not comfortable with. In addition, this can complicate your life in far many ways. One of the best ways to fight away your phobias is through hypnosis. This exercise helps you overcome your fears and start living in a healthy fashion.

Eliminating PTSD

People go through a lot of emotional pain on a daily basis. You only need to turn the news in order to see how people are suffering around the world. It does not matter how lofty one might be in society, but they have been traumatized in one way or another. These tough experiences that we go through leave us emotionally broken. They leave us traumatized. In addition, this usually predisposes us to post-traumatic stress disorder. One of the ways to get rid of PTSD is through hypnosis. Performing this exercise on the regular helps, us gain understanding as to what we really are, the root cause of our emotional disturbance, and helps us gain awareness of how to put our emotional vulnerabilities in check.

Fighting Off Dysfunctions

One of the worst conditions that could plague a human being is a dysfunction. It simply means that one cannot perform as they are expected to. Having dysfunctions of any kind can take away the pleasures of life. In addition, this causes the person in question to become dissatisfied with the quality of their life. Overcoming a dysfunction is not something you would achieve in a snap of a finger. However, performing hypnosis on the regular has been proven to help people overcome their dysfunctions and start leading their best possible lives.

Eliminating Relationships Issues

A famous man once said that in order to be happy, one needs work to do, and someone to love. As human beings, we cannot get away from love, because it is the main point of living. However, far often, we find ourselves with the wrong person. We get into abusive relationships and hey ruin our self-esteem. Then sometimes we get into relationships that are perfect in the beginning only to grow worse at a later time. If we are paired with the right person, but due to our negative habits or mindset we start ruining the relationship. It makes sense to salvage the relationship instead of throwing it away. Hypnosis can help people come back into being the best partner and this allows them to have a powerful relationship going.

Settling Family Issues

Most people will tell you that their family comes first. However, if you would take a close look at most families, you would notice patterns that give rise to conflict. As human beings, conflict is just one decision away. Just because a family is, having problems does not mean that the whole family is helpless. It is rather an opportunity for the family members to work out their differences and start leading their best lives. Hypnosis is one of the exercises that helps fight away their family issues.

How to Find People Who Are Easy to Hypnotize?

Hypnosis is guarded by a number of principles. Once you observe these principles, your target should fall under your power, so that you can plant suggestions into their mind. Then the capacity for people to be hypnotized differs. Some people are easy to hypnotize and others are not so easy. In order to be successful in your efforts, you have to first profile your target, so that you are sure they are easy to hypnotize, for this makes your work a lot easier. The following are some of the factors that point to people who are easy to hypnotize.

They like Fantasy

If someone is captivated by the world of fantasy, they are a good candidate for hypnotism. One needs to have an active imagination for the best chances. In addition, someone who is into having fantasies or enjoys fantasy-related things is likely to have a high imaginative drive. It is important to have a conversation with this person as you try to find out who they really are as it gives you a glimpse into whether or not they are inclined to fantasy-ridden ideals. The more a person is into fantasy, the better candidate they are for hypnosis.

Having Strict Parents

In your interactions with your target, you might want to find out what their parents were like. Generally, someone who had strict parents has grown into someone who follows instruction pretty easily, and that makes them a better candidate for hypnosis, as opposed to someone whose parents were never there for them. When you really think about it, hypnosis is about issuing instructions, making the person assimilate your ideas, and if they had strict parents, it means they are not new to receiving instructions.

Age

Technically, hypnosis flies better with extremes in terms of age i.e. People who are either on the young side or the elderly side. This is not to mean that any other person cannot fall into the power of hypnosis; but rather, it works better with people who are either young or elderly.

However, the greatest determinant of success in hypnosis is the observance of the principles. Ensure that you are following the rules and it doesn't matter who your target might be, but they will fall into your power.

Chapter 10 What Is The Dark Triad Psychology? (Narcissism, Machiavellianism, And Psychopathy)

The Dark Triad

Another area of importance in the world of psychology, is the Dark Triad. The Dark Triad is a set of three particular personality traits that are associated with some not so great things. As noted, they are Psychopathy, Narcissism, and Machiavellianism. Each of these traits have their own set of characteristics. Let's take a minute and look at each one to gain a better understanding of why they are considered dark.

We have all met people in our lives that are narcissistic or that others refer to as narcissists. A person who has the traits of Narcissism is one that thinks a lot of themselves. It is not always thinking you are the most beautiful one in the room, however, many narcissists do find themselves to be insanely attractive.

Narcissists are also, commonly, people who have giant egos. They have a totally unrealistic view on their personal image. Obviously, people that are too full of themselves are difficult to be around and tend to be great at manipulation people and situations. Pretty easy to see why this is a character trait that we, non-narcissist, are happy to not have.

Psychopathy has its own traits and they are much different than that of the Narcissist. Psychopathy is characterized by exceptionally anti-social behaviors. The psychopath does not, typically, feel empathy toward others. In addition, they can have big egos and no remorse for their actions in life. Unlike sociopaths who tend to come unhinged easily, Psychopaths are calculated and oftentimes very charming. This makes them dangerous.

Machiavellianism, or "High Mech", is the master of all manipulators. They don't choose to be that way, they simply are that way. This type of person will go to extremes to gain power. Lying, cheating, stealing, and treachery are nothing to them. If the choice is between doing something moral to eventually meet your goals or stepping on and deceiving people to achieve goals more quickly, they will choose the latter every time. High Mech's are calculating. They can be charming, but they will also use guilt and pressure to get what they want.

When it comes down to it people that are part of the Dark Triad will do just about anything in their power to get what they want. You can easily see why this is dangerous and detrimental to the people around them. Having the ability to recognize these traits in people can help to keep you protected from their poison.

It's crazy to think how difficult it would be to deal with someone with only one of these issues. If you are around, in love, or working with one that falls into all three categories it can cause serious damage to your mental health. Hopefully, with more understanding those of you that deal with this type of behavior will be better prepared.

Criminology

Dark Psychology and Psychology play major roles in the world of Criminology. When you are trying to catch a criminal, it is easier if you understand how they think. Therefore, it is easy to see why these three things go hand in hand. Getting into the mind of a criminal, killer, or rapist can be very difficult for those of us that do not have these extremely dark tendencies. So, the fact that there is information accumulating for us to research is critical.

It is hard to wrap your brain around how a human being can be wired so much differently. Until we find the ability to do this, it can make catching the really bad guys difficult. With advances in understanding the darker tendencies of human nature it has become easier for Criminologists, Police Officers, and others to find these ugly individuals.

Psychology, and in turn, Dark Psychology have been around for a very long time. In fact, as far back as histories go, there have been people working on understanding why humans do what they do. We all have the capability of doing bad things. Some of us have a much easier time doing these non-moral acts above others.

Finding examples of people from the past to present day that have the qualities studied in Dark Psychology is easy. It doesn't matter what time frame you look at you will be able to pick out the characteristics easily with a few, obvious examples. Once you see it on a large scale you can start to look at the people around you every day and see some of the same features. It is actually quite unsettling to realize how many people around you are prone to dark desires.

One of the most obvious examples is Adolf Hitler. Obviously, he committed awful acts. However, he had more than an entire country under his thumb. Why is that? Well, he was charismatic, he spoke articulately, and he was an amazing manipulator. He completely understood what he needed to do to have control over the masses.

He built a core group of like-minded people to help him along the way. While these people had a better look at what the truth was behind his tactics, we can't believe they knew everything. A person such as Adolf Hitler would never let all of their secrets out. When looking for a prime example of a person that falls into all three categories of the Dark Triad, he is perfect.

With fear, power, charisma, likability, and laser focus he managed to convince his people to commit atrocious acts against humanity. It's odd to think that on an individual level, his followers were normal good people. When bombarded with propaganda, well-thought out words, and intimidation they bent to the will of a madman.

If people were better able to understand what was driving Hitler, there could have been a stop to his reign much more quickly.

With more information in Dark Psychology, pinpointing the traits of a person like Hitler is easier than ever.

Another great example of a person that truly tapped into their dark nature was, cult leader, James Warren Jones. More commonly referred to as Jim Jones. Many people are familiar with the phrase "drinking the Kool Aid" and we have him to thank for that. He ran a cult that consisted of around 900 people. They all, literally, worshiped him.

His cult was called The People's Temple. He made promises of a Utopia for all of his followers. He relied on his charismatic attitude, well-spoken words, manipulation, and deceit to rope a large group of people to his calling.

From the outside, he appeared to be doing and saying things for all the right reasons. He was vocal about issues like racial integration and homelessness. He truly looked like a man of god with good intentions. This was heinously inaccurate. He was after power and control at any means necessary.

Once he had amassed a serious following, he relocated everyone to Guyana. Here, he started to rule his cult a bit differently. Instead of appearing like someone who was doing righteous acts he started to manipulate his followers in a more obviously dark way. He would use threats of physical violence, blackmail, and even death to control the people that were following him.

Most people are pretty familiar with how this story ends. Upon worrying that the authorities were going to become involved with what was going on in Jonestown, he coerced his following to drink arsenic clad punch. His dark nature prevailed, and they did indeed drink the Kool Aid, which resulted in 900 deaths that included men, women, and children.

One last great example of a person pursuing nothing, but power is seen in Delphine LaLaurie. Some people have probably never heard of this woman and many wishes that they had not. When you are looking for someone that seeks total control over people and takes pleasure in their pain, she is the person you should look toward.

Born as Marie Delphine Macarty, this southern socialite married a few different men in the course of her life. Eventually, she was simply known as Madam LaLaurie. She maintained a great standing with the people of New Orleans. She was very in touch with everything that was going on and people held her in seriously high-regard. Little did they know something much more sinister was going on behind the scenes.

LaLaurie owned more slaves than most other people and she loved to torture them. With little to no reasoning she would perform awful acts against them to show true dominance. Oftentimes, it led to months of torture for these poor souls, just to be ended in death. What LaLaurie looked like to the common public and what she really was were two completely different things.

Dark factor (D-factor)

There are core attributes that are sharable between the three key personality types that comprise the Dark Triad.

These core attributes are collectively referred to as the Dark Factor. The Dark Factor is the key driver of the Dark Psychology.

In essence, the Dark factor refers to the malevolent dark sides of human personality characterized by the following 9 key traits:

Egoism

Self-interest

Psychological entitlement

Moral disengagement

Spitefulness

Sadism

Machiavellianism

Narcissism

Psychopathy

Egoism

Egoism is characterized by excessive preoccupation with own gains regardless of the cost, loss, or pain inflicted on others. In egoism, the anti-cathexis is such weak that the super-ego lacks and Id predominates.

Self-interest

Self-interest is characterized by a strong desire to achieve and exhibit one's own social and financial status.

Psychological entitlement

Psychological entitlement is a persistent tendency by one to perceive oneself as being better than others and thus deserving of better treatment.

Moral disengagement

Moral disengagement is a cognitive processing style which permits one to indulge oneself in unethical conduct without any sense of distress (such as guilt or remorse).

Spitefulness

Spitefulness is the destructive willingness to inflict harm on others irrespective of being harmed in the process.

Sadism

Sadism is a tendency to achieve desirous pleasure from the act of inflicting harm on others whether be it for personal gain or not.

Machiavellianism

Machiavellianism is a highly callous and manipulative attitude anchored on the belief that the end justifies the means.

Narcissism

Narcissism is the predisposition towards excessive self-absorption resulting in a heightened false sense of superiority and unbridled desire for excessive attention from others.

Psychopathy

Psychopathy is an absolute lack of empathy accompanied by lack of self-control, which results in highly impulsive behavior.

Machiavellian personality type

Machiavellian personality type is by far the most dominant personality type. It is more of a learned form of personality type. As such, it is considered a normal occurrence in society. For example, most politicians are Machiavellian by nature. Similarly, a good number of religious characters are Machiavellian by nature. So, it is one of the most normalized personality types despite its dark source.

Furthermore, Machiavellianism is the only personality type within the Dark triad that does not have any pathological extreme.

The following are key attributes of the Machiavellian personality type:

Very deceptive

Low regard for others

Taking advantage of others to achieve own self-interest

Low empathetic concern for others

Highly manipulative

Highly uncooperative

Low levels of moral ethics

Compulsive

Highly initiative

Risk-taker in seeking new opportunities

Pleasure-seeking

While high-risk takers, they are highly strategic, prudent and guarded in protecting their gains.

Although extremely impulsive in making quick decisions, they are capable of making cold-minded decisions (free from emotional impulses) in the long-term strategy

Fear of fusion (that is, fear of being emotionally attached to others)

Narcissistic personality type

Narcissistic personality type is probably the second most dominant of the three personality types within the Dark triad.

The following are the key characteristics of a narcissistic personality type:

Self-imputation of superiority

Epiphanic knowledge

Infallibility

Assumption that others crave for their knowledge and wisdom

Monopolistic tendencies to possess and isolate those around them from the rest of the populace

False modesty

Only gifts the sources of his narcissistic supply

Use of projection as a psychological defense mechanism

They exhibit dissociative gap and confabulation

Consider themselves to be above the law

Disruptive

Resent authority

Counter-dependent

Hold themselves immune to the consequences of their actions

They exhibit narcissistic rage

They are ill-disposed towards criticism and disagreement

Types of narcissists:

Overt (straight) narcissists

Covert (inverted) narcissists

Malignant narcissists

Types of narcissism

Pathological narcissism

Healthy (therapeutic) narcissism

Psychopathic personality type

Psychopathic personality type is the least common of the three personality types within the Dark triad. However, it is also the most severe of them all. Its potency can be extremely dangerous when blend with narcissism and/or Machiavellianism.

Joseph Stalin is probably the best typical example that embodied the optimal combination of the three personality types within the Dark triad, by which they converged into a grandeur and dangerous personality.

The following are some of the main traits of psychopathic personality type:

Big risk-takers

Fearless

Highly deceptive

Serious lack of empathy

Cold-hearted

Callous

Extremely arrogant

Highly superficial charm

Lack remorse

Master manipulators

Extremely poor judgment – they hardly learn from past punishment

Egocentric and unable to establish long-term loving relationships

Glibness

High sense of self-importance

Chapter 11 Dark Triad Axis and Application

Narcissistic Actions and Their Applications

The narcissist introduction to manipulation stems from their need to preserve their self-esteem. By their nature, a narcissist will inflate their own ego through the emotional manipulation and abuse of those around them. To keep an air of superiority, they have to bring everyone around them down constantly.

Because of this, a narcissist will regard other people as extensions of themselves. Where a regular person sees a waiter trying to make an honest living, a narcissist sees a servant. Everyone that the narcissist encounters exists to serve them in some way. They can exploit their freedoms through the disregard of the targets wants and desires, or denigrate them emotionally to gain a self-confidence boost.

A narcissist is a user of people, and to get there, they need to use dark psychology. Narcissist parents can cause a substantial amount of emotional damage to their children, and may sometimes do so willingly through manipulation and gaslighting. Here the narcissist wants to attack those closest to them in order to feel better about themselves.

One doesn't have to be a narcissist to appreciate the why's of such behavior. Everyone wants to feel better about themselves, especially people who suffer from low self-esteem. A sort of narrow narcissism can be applied to oneself, boosting the level of self-importance as an exercise in confidence creation.

Gaining the confidence to use dark psychology is often a first step in going down the manipulation route. Narrow narcissism can help reach this place. A true narcissist does not care about the feelings or goals of other people, so using dark psychology for them is like second nature.

A narcissist is also self-preserving. Nothing hurts more than the thought that they can one day die, and no longer be the center of the attention. To compensate, they will direct attention towards themselves at all times and constantly inflate their self-importance when they feel it is deflating. They use similar tactics to that of defensive gaslighting—manipulative techniques intended to defend the manipulator from suspicion. In the case of the narcissist, it is not their manipulation that they are trying to hide, but their fragile sense of arrogance.

An understanding of the narcissist and why their actions do deplorable provides a basis for the future trust-building of new targets. A narcissist is usually easier to spot than any other type of manipulator if they don't go through the pains of hiding it. A narcissist is always "me, me, me" and that can get boring fast.

A stronger manipulator, like that of a psychopath, understands what people want and are willing to show people only what they want. The narcissist just wants to run people over. And in many cases, they have the direct authority and the necessary power relationship (like a parent and an underage child) to do so.

But acting like a narcissist in the wild will not get you many takers. The trick is to act in opposition to what the narcissist would do. Where the narcissist would look only after themselves, an experienced manipulator must firs cater to the target. This includes in all manner of speech, charitable actions, and especially when it comes to doing favors.

A narcissist can often be spotted simply by the way they conduct themselves in speech. Because they can't go long without talking about their own importance, they will often ignore the needs of others (or simply not realize that others have needs). In everyday conversation, this can be rather scathing.

Below is an example of a narcissistic conversation and an example of a normal, supportive conversation.

"I am having such a bad today. You wouldn't imagine what I've been through"

"Man, bad days are such a drag. I'm having a really good day today. Did I tell you about the perfect dress I picked up earlier?"

"I am having such a bad today. You wouldn't imagine what I've been through"

"I'm sorry to hear you are having a bad day. What happened?"

A good manipulator understands that their target has immediate needs that need to be fulfilled if they intend to continue the relationship for a while. Building trust is important, and it is something that the true narcissist struggles with.

Machiavellian Actions and Their Applications

Machiavellian has obvious applications to dark psychology. This has to do mostly with the aspect of dealing in the shadows and not making an attacker's intentions known. The grand Machiavellian scheme can be summed up in the deception campaigns that the attacker uses to trick their targets into trusting them.

It also applies to the ruthless nature of dark psychology tactics. Doing everything that is possible to reach one's goals is very much the attitude that many manipulators adopt. Though the major difference is that the use of force isn't always used, as this defeats the purpose of using dark psychology in the first place.

A Machiavellian action is lying to someone's face fully knowing that this person trusts you. When a politician makes a promise just for the purpose of getting a reaction, they are doing the same thing. They may or may not be willing to fulfill that promise, but they are definitely pandering to a larger political agenda.

Every manipulator has its own unique agenda they are looking to make a reality. Manipulation is really just a tool for realizing it. Some will enter a new relationship with a potential target already knowing what this agenda is. They hatch the Machiavellian scheme inside of their heads and base all further actions around it.

In the workplace, Machiavellianism is routinely used to get ahead. In a world were promotions are limited, and the desire to have a better paying position endless, employees muscle for rank. Though some prefer to operate in the shadows, these are the types that start rumors, talk behind the backs of their fellow employees, and kiss up to their superiors.

They are also the same people who will rat another employee out in an instant, even if it means reporting someone who was simply slacking off. Still, others may decide to lay traps in the workplace like sabotaging work orders, messing with machinery, and causing interpersonal drama.

All things being equal, somebody who uses Machiavellianism has an advantage over the person who does not. Going into an interview and being completely honest may not be as effective as embellishing a few details here and there, and maybe creating work histories on the fly.

Psychopathic Actions and Their Applications

Psychopathy is really the holy grail of dark psychology. It is at the apex of both narcissism and Machiavellianism but with select differences. A psychopath is a callous, murderous, and relentless entity that will stop at nothing to get what they want—usually money and status. They also have a thing for power over others. They live to control, subvert, and to subjugate their targets.

But psychopaths need not be murderers, kidnappers or rapist (though a fair number of them are). They could be your boss, a teacher, a coworker, or even your next-door neighbor. The population of those with enough psychopathic traits to be considered psychopaths is around 1%. That means for every million people in the population; there are some 10,000 psychopaths walking around, which is sort of a lot considering what a psychopath is capable.

Someone who deals with a narcissist frequently knows that they are not pleasant people. They are obnoxious, abrasive, and with little social graces. A psychopath, on the other hand, is a born people-pleaser in disguise. They are charming above all and like to disarm people early in their relationship.

A psychopath has a smooth exterior, which is ideal for building trust in others. Inside they are cold and calculating, with several gears going at the same time. None of these gears are concerned with humanitarianism. If they need to hurt someone, either physically or emotionally, to get what they need, then they will.

Psychopaths are also narcissists by nature, but they are able to hide this aspect in favor of being their charming self. A psychopath is still out for them and only them. While they might help people in the short term, an action is only taken if they perceive that it will benefit them the most when all is said and done.

These characteristics make the psychopath an ideal candidate for mimicking in a dark psychology attack. First is the charming exterior, and the second is the Machiavellian scheme to carry out. And of course, the self-interest that only a narcissist could possess.

Knowing this, the person dabbling in dark psychology needs to understand where these techniques come from. They come from the dark triad, and psychopathy in particular. Anyone who is willing to resort to dark psychology for personal gain must also be willing to delve in narcissism, Machiavellianism, and psychopathy.

Using dark psychology doesn't make a person any of these things, but it does require that they act in the same way, at least until the manipulation has been completed. For many, this is a tall order to complete and will refuse to adopt some of these traits. As a consequence, their manipulations are not very successful.

The question to ask is, what would a psychopath do? Would a psychopath use physical force to coerce somebody against their will? Maybe. But most likely, a psychopath will use a combination of superficial charm and shrewd manipulation to do the same.

Chapter 12 Speed Reading People

What Is Speeding People?

Ignite the Art of Reading People through Your Super Senses

If you want to read people, you have to don the garment of a psychiatrist who has the power to interpret cues which are verbal and nonverbal. You need to observe beyond people's masks into their real self. You may not get the entire picture about anybody through logic alone. You have to surrender to their critical forms of information to interpret the essential nonverbal perceptive cues that individuals exude. For you to achieve this feat, you need to be eager to surrender emotional baggage like ego clashes or old resentments and also any preconceptions which can prevent you from making out the person. It is crucial, as well, for you to obtain information without bias and continue to be impartial without twisting it.

In the process of reading a colleague, your boss, or partner for you to understand them accurately, some walls need to come down, and you need to surrender biases. You need to be ready to let go of limiting, old ideas as far as intellect is concerned. Those who read other people well are taught to comprehend the hidden. They have discovered how they will draw on what is called 'super-sense' so they can take a profound observation beyond where you usually steer your focus when you attempt to hack into transformative awareness.

Examine cues of body language

When you are reading the cues of body language, you have to surrender the focus by releasing your struggle to understand the hidden signals of body language. Never get analytical or overtly intense. Stay fluid and relaxed. Observe by sitting back comfortably.

Focus on appearance

When you are reading other people, take note of what they are wearing. Are they putting on well-shined shoes and power suit? The indication for success is when someone deck out decently. For someone wearing a T-shirt and jeans may be an indicator of that person being comfortable with casual. It may be a signal of a seductive choice when someone wears a tight top with cleavage. A pendant like Buddha or cross may indicate spiritual values.

Notice posture

Postures are an essential aspect of reading people. It's a sign of confident when people's head is held high. Or you can get an indication of low self-esteem when they cower, or they walk irresolutely. You can also get a sign of a big ego when they have puffed-out chest and swagger.

Pay attention to physical movements

When you read others, look out for their distance and learning. In general, people bend forward at those they like and keep a distance from others they don't. Also, when people cross their arms and legs, you can see signs of anger, self-protection, or defensiveness. It is an indication that people are hiding something when they hide their hands by placing them in their pockets, laps, or place them behind them. With cuticle picking or lip biting, you will get a sign of people attempting to calm themselves in a difficult circumstance or under pressure.

Read facial expression

Our faces provide the outline for our emotions. Profound frown lines indicate over-thinking or worry. The smile lines of delight are crow's feet; pursed lips is a signal of contempt, anger, or bitterness. While teeth grinding and clenched jaw are indicators of tension.

Take note to your intuition

It is possible to tune into someone ahead of their words and body language. Though not what your head says, what your gut feels is intuition. Instead of logic, intuition is your perception of nonverbal information through images. If you are in the process of understanding a person, their outer trappings are insignificant, and it is only who the person is what counts. To reveal a richer story, intuition gives the power to distinguish beyond the obvious to tell a richer story.

You need to watch out for these checklists cues of intuition:

Respect your gut feelings

Pay attention to voices of your gut, in particular when connecting with someone for the first time, an automatic rejoinder that happens out of impulse. Gut feelings are as a result of if you are tensed up or at ease. As a cardinal response, gut feelings occur in an instant. They are meters of your inner truth that relay to you if you should trust someone.

Goosebumps feelings

Pleasant, intuitive shivers are goosebumps, and they happen when something strikes a chord in us in connection with our resonance to individuals that inspire or move us. Also, goosebumps occur in the course of going through déjà-vu and when you have never met someone before but still recognize them.

Listen to sparkles of insight

During a conversation with people, you may be impressed by those who come quickly. Watch out and stay alert. Or else, you might fail to spot it. For most of us, this crucial awareness is lost because of the inclination to move onto the next idea.

Look for insightful empathy

This cue happens when you have a passionate type of empathy through the feelings of someone's real emotions and symptoms within your body. So, while reading people, take note whether you had pain on your back when it wasn't there before, or if you are upset or depressed following a mind-numbing conference. To determine if empathy is at play, get feedback.

Discern emotional power

The vibe we radiate and the remarkable demonstration of our energy are emotions. It is with an intuition that we procure these emotions. For some people, you will be happy to be around them because they enhance your vitality and mood. Others tend to be draining; get away from them is what you want. Though it is undetectable, you can feel this 'subtle energy' feet or inches from the body. It's called **chi** in Chinese medicine, an essential healthy vitality.

Be aware of the presence of people

Though not substantially similar to our behavior or words, the accustomed energy we discharge is when we sense the presence of the people. It is typical of a rain cloud or the sun that borders around our emotional atmosphere. In the process of reading people, take note of if you get attraction with their presence or retreating due to the willies you are getting.

Watch people's eyes

Humans' eyes convey compelling forces. As the eyes cast off an electromagnetic signal, according to studies, the brain does the same. When you watch people's eyes, you will know if they are tranquil, sexy, mean, angry, or caring. Also, you will have the ability to determine if a person wants intimacy in their eyes or their eyes can give signs that they are comfortable. Even in their eyes, you will know whether they appear to be hiding or guarded.

Observe the feel of a hug, handshake, or touch

Most of us shake emotional energy, similar to an electrical flow during physical contact. You can ask yourself if a hug or handshake feel comfortable, warm, or confident. Or if it is repulsive so much that you wish to withdraw. You can know the sign of anxiety with someone's hand clammy or limp to suggest being timid or non-committal.

Listen to the tone of laugh and voice

Our voice's volume and tone are capable of telling a lot about our emotions. Vibration is as a result of sound frequencies. Notice how people's pitch of voice affects you in the course of reading them. Envisage if the tone is snippy, abrasive, and whiny or if their tone feels soothing.

To read people can be hard sometimes. It takes practice and courage. However, once you are past that, you will gain a significant advantage. Not only will you survive, but you will also thrive in all your relationships with others. People will approach you. Opportunities will come to you. And some people will want to be like you.

Conclusion

When a person is persuaded or manipulated into doing something that is beneficial to them, they don't feel overwhelmed but when they feel shortchanged, it can be devastating. If this has been your feeling, then the good news is you do not have to feel it again.

The book has given you great tips and exercises that you can use to overcome manipulation. After reading this book, you will now be able to spot manipulation and avoid it. The book also guides you on how you can manipulate others as well. If you have been finding difficulties in closing deals or convincing others, it is now much easier to influence and get your way.

With the excellent tips and strategies shared in the book, you will not only be able to overcome mind control, but you will be able to use it to your advantage. The modern technique of manipulation in NLP can help you to achieve your objectives no matter what they are.

Now that you know how persuasion can be powerful, use it to your advantage from today. As an individual, you can also persuade yourself to achieve what you want through manipulating your subconscious mind. The mind is indeed a powerful tool that if well used, one can achieve great success.

Create burning desires and go out to achieve them as articulated in the book. You can now be able to spot and identify victims of manipulation and help stop it.

You want to achieve greatness, use the tips shared in this book. You have seen some of the most famous people in the world and how they used manipulation to their advantage. You too can benefit from the tips and strategies in this book. Follow the examples shared in the book and notice your life change.

Thanks for reading this book. I really hope it has left you some valuable notions to exploit in everyday life;

I wish you all the best!